Sea Raptors

Logs of the Private Armed Vessels
Comet and *Chasseur*
Commanded by Tom Boyle

1812-1815

BATTLE between the BRIG CHASSEUR and the SCHOONER St. LAWRENCE off Havanna on the 26th of Feb. 1815

Compiled and Annotated by
Andrew J. Wahll

HERITAGE BOOKS
2008

HERITAGE BOOKS
AN IMPRINT OF HERITAGE BOOKS, INC.

Books, CDs, and more—Worldwide

For our listing of thousands of titles see our website at
www.HeritageBooks.com

Published 2008 by
HERITAGE BOOKS, INC.
Publishing Division
100 Railroad Ave. #104
Westminster, Maryland 21157

Copyright © 2008 Andrew J. Wahll

Other books by the author:

Braddock Road Chronicles, 1755 (from the Diaries and Records of Members of the Braddock Expedition and Others Arranged in a Day by Day Chronology)

Henry Mowat: Voyage of the Canceaux, 1764-1776: Abridged Logs of H. M. Armed Ship Canceaux

Sabino, Popham Colony (Maine) Reader: 1602-2003

All rights reserved. No part of this book may be reproduced or transmitted in any form or by any means, electronic or mechanical, including photocopying, recording or by any information storage and retrieval system without written permission from the author, except for the inclusion of brief quotations in a review.

International Standard Book Numbers
Paperbound: 978-0-7884-4371-8
Clothbound: 978-0-7884-7221-3

Contents

Acknowledgments v
Introduction vii
Overview of Atlantic Naval Operations in the War of 1812..1
Documents:
    Department of the Navy Pension Entitlement Notice 3
    Department of State Presidential Order 4
Cruises of the *Comet* 5
1811 Background 6
1812 Background 7
Log of the *Comet*
    First Voyage, July 1812–November 1812 9
1813 Background 14
Log of the *Comet*
    Second Voyage, November 1812–October 1813 15
Log of the *Comet*
    Third Voyage, October 1813–March 1814 26
Overview of the Campaign on the Atlantic Coast and
    Chesapeake Bay 34
Chasseur Articles of Agreement, including list of officers and
    men 45
Journal of Private Armed Brig *Chasseur* by Thos. Boyle,
    Commander, December 1814–March 1815 53
1815 Overview 55
Log of *Chasseur*, December 23, 1815–March 17, 1815 56
Court Martial of Lt. James Edward Gordon and Surviving
    Officers and Crew of H.M.S. *St. Lawrence* 87
After Action Letters, Accounts and Reports *Chasseur/HMS
    St. Lawrence*, from *Niles Weekly Register* 97
List of Private Armed Vessels out of Baltimore and their
    Prizes, 1812–1815 103

Notes 106
Appendix 117
"Sketch of the Gallant Achievements of the Heroic Captain Thomas Boyle, of the Privateer Brig *Chasseur*," from *History of the American Privateers and Letters-of-Marque* by George Coggeshall 117
"Arrival of the Privateer Chasseur," from *A History of American Privateers* by Edgar Stanton Maclay 120
List of Vessels noted in the logs of the *Comet* and *Chasseur* 123
List of Privateers from Baltimore and New York 124
Glossary 125
Sources 141
Index 145

Acknowledgments

Scott Sheads, (National Park Service, Fort McHenry); Jerome Bird and Captain Jan Miles (*Pride of Baltimore*); Elisabeth Proffin (Maryland Historical Society); Donald Showmette; Geoffrey Footner; Mike Crawford (Naval History Center); Christopher George; Ed Nelson (Maryland Historical Society); Beatriz B. Hardy (Maryland Historical Society); Richard Cottom; Dennis Conrad (Naval History Center); Janet MacDonald (Naval History Center); John Berg; Chris Freeman; Don Seltzer; St. Mary's County, Maryland, Historical Society; Prince George's County, Maryland, Public Library; Robert O'Hara, London, England, researcher (searcher@diron.co.uk); and Public Record Office, London, England.

Introduction

Naval historian Ben Lankford wrote:

> A type of sailing vessel known as the Baltimore Clipper first appeared during the American Revolution. Because the ship was so fast, its hull design became a favorite and was patterned after by privateers, slavers, and others desiring rapid transportation on the sea. The Baltimore Clipper was fully developed and most successful during the period from 1805 to 1815 and is generally accepted as the precursor to the clipper ship era of the 1850's. It was as a privateer during the War of 1812 that the Baltimore Clipper became most famous. With sleek lines and few guns, the Baltimore Clippers were light and exceptionally fast. Their maneuverability made it possible to wreak havoc on the British; the speedy privateers could overtake and outrun the enemy with ease, and this enabled the privateer owners to take large profits from the many prizes they seized. When the war ended in 1815 with the Treaty of Ghent, the number of this type of ship began to diminish. Many of the schooners were sold to South American and Caribbean owners. By 1860, the Baltimore Clipper was gone.
>
> During the 17th and 18th centuries, the waterways of the Chesapeake Bay provided an excellent home and work environment for the early settlers. The overseas demand for tobacco and new ships kept the area alive with commerce. Many talented shipwrights plied their trade at the numerous shipyards located on the Eastern Shore. One in particular, Thomas Kemp, departed for Baltimore and Fells Point in 1803 to seek his fortune and avoid the local competition. Establishing himself as a leader, he built many fast and notorious Baltimore Clippers. With the newly independent America's need to establish itself in European trade, and develop militarily on the open seas,

his success was immediate, and paved the way for others who migrated north.

Because Baltimore had the investment capital, it could provide the higher wages that eventually drew the best builders and craftsmen, as well as the many excellent captains and sailors required to man the ships. With the turning away from shipping tobacco to the major export of flour, Baltimore became one of the most productive shipbuilding and shipping centers of the time.

Although the ship type had been fully developed, the name Baltimore Clipper was not applied to it until the ship was almost extinct. The type was once called a Baltimore Flyer, and early records simply refer to it as a Virginia Built Boat, or Fast Sailing Schooner, light and sleek, fast and seaworthy, it was a topsail schooner with extremely raked masts. It had a wide, flush deck to allow easy handling of the ship, and when fitted as a privateer, it had guns. The type seems to have developed from the Chesapeake Bay sloop soon found to be too small.

The Baltimore Clipper carved out a place for itself in history. The schooner facilitated the nation's ability to win independence and they helped the city of Baltimore establish its identity as a major shipbuilding center.

—Found in an instruction manual for the construction of a model of *Pride of Baltimore II* (1988) prepared by Model Shipways

The intent of this book is to highlight privateering activity of Chesapeake Bay mariners during the War of 1812 by exploring chronologically the logs of the vessels *Comet* and *Chasseur,* under command of Captain Tom Boyle.

As a guide to the reader, the sequences of logs appearing in this book are as follows:

Log of the *Comet,* First Voyage (July 1812–Nov. 1812)
Log of the *Comet,* Second Voyage (Nov. 1812–Oct. 1813)
Log of the *Comet,* Third Voyage (Oct. 1813–March 1814)
Log of the *Chasseur* (Dec. 1814–March 1815)

Introduction ix

As we near the 200th anniversary of the War of 1812 these records will be of great interest to the people of the Chesapeake region. The *Chasseur* was designed and built by Thomas Kemp, a prolific craftsman who also built the privateers *Rossie* and *Rolla*.[1] Kemp arrived at Fells Point from Talbot County, Maryland, in 1803. He bought property at Fells Point and built his shipyard on a lot bounded by Fleet, Washington, and Fountain Streets in Fells Point. *Comet* and *Chasseur* were both built at this yard in 1810. *Comet* was launched at Noon (Meridian). The second vessel was launched at 4 P.M. on December 12, 1812. It was christened the *Chasseur* and was later popularly called *The Pride of Baltimore*. The *Chasseur* was an inch short of 116 feet long and had a weight of 356 tons unburdened. She was the largest private armed vessel to be built and commissioned at Fells Point. The name, *Pride of Baltimore*, has been used in our times for two sailing replicas of the vessel used in a variety of educational programs and as a goodwill ambassador on the international marine scene. The first of the modern vessels was launched on February 27, 1977, and sank in hurricane winds on its return voyage from St. Thomas on May 14, 1986, with the loss of four crew members. The second vessel, called the *Pride of Baltimore II,* was launched on April 30, 1988.

William Dudley, in *The Naval War of 1812: A Documentary History*, comments about the subject of privateering:

> The typical privateer ship of the War of 1812 was a fast-sailing schooner or brig out of Salem[2] or Baltimore,[3] heavily armed and carrying a large crew. Ship owners drafted their captains' orders and expected that they would operate independently of other ships. Privateers did not usually choose to fight a British warship, and it was considered no disgrace to run from such an encounter when the odds were dubious. Owners, captain, and crew shared unequally in the proceeds of a successful capture. When possible, prize crews were placed on board captured vessels, and they were directed to sail to the nearest safe port where the prizes could be libeled[4] and condemned in an Admiralty Court proceeding.[5] After judgment,[6] the ship

and goods were put up for sale, and the proceeds went to the owners who received a fifty percent share. The remainder was then distributed to captain, officers, and crew of the privateer in accordance with the articles of agreement signed before the voyage.

This log-based narrative follows the events of Tom Boyle's privateering career aboard two American vessels (*Comet* and *Chasseur*) during our second war for independence.

Fred W. Hopkins, Jr. writes in, *Tom Boyle, Master Privateer,* that Boyle had an early association with maritime interests in Baltimore beginning in 1792, when his name was listed in the Baltimore Registry of Ships as master of the schooner *Hester,* owned by John Carrere. In 1793, the seventeen-year-old Boyle was in command of the ship *Theresa,* newly built for John Carrere, followed by the Carrere-owned schooner *Providence*. After marrying Mary Gross[7] in 1794, Boyle was back at sea eleven days later commanding the schooner *Expedition*. Five years later in 1797 he was in command of the second vessel with the name of *Theresa*. In 1798 he commanded the *Vigilant,* followed in 1802 by another vessel by the same name. In 1803 Boyle became part owner of *Cordelia* with Mr. Carrere. In 1804 Boyle was sole owner and master of his own vessel, a brig called *Traveller*. Then in 1806 he is listed as owner of the brig *Greenwich* followed by the schooner *Sally*.[8] The next entry in the Customs House registry for Boyle is five years later, when he took command of the *Comet* in the year 1812.

On June 18, 1812, President James Madison declared America's "second war of independence" against England. Hopkins points out that "hostilities gave ship owners and masters the opportunity to practice one of the more profitable aspects of waging war at sea: privateering." Baltimore became one of the centers of this enterprise, where owners rushed to arm their fastest schooners and brigs and get them to sea to raid British commerce.

Part of this narrative is the coming together in deadly combat of two opposing American-built topsail schooners in a classical sea battle with salvos in broadside fashion and the resultant bloodwashed scuppers of an American victory. The *Atlas,* a private armed schooner from St. Michael's in Talbot County, Maryland, was captured by the British squadron at Okracoke Inlet, North Carolina. It was repaired and fitted out as a raider at Bermuda in his Britannic Majesty's Navy.

The logs presented here have been published elsewhere, however, this volume presents the many additional historic writings and interpretations pertaining to the exploits of Tom Boyle and his ships. The court martial of James Edward Gordon, Captain of H.M.S. *St. Lawrence,* appears in print for the first time. As Cranwell and Crane observed, "Tom Boyle aboard the *Comet* was the epitome of privateering, but Tom Boyle aboard the *Chasseur* was its apotheosis."

[1] The *Rossie* was built in 1807, the *Rolla* in 1809.
[2] This is the port of Salem, Massachusetts, home port of 40 privateers.
[3] Home port to 58 privateers.
[4] The written claims by a plaintiff in an action at admiralty law.
[5] A court exercising jurisdiction over all maritime causes.
[6] A determination of a court of law.
[7] *Pride of Baltimore: Renaissance of the Baltimore Clipper* (Baltimore Operation Sail, Ltd., 1977) calls his bride Polly Gross.
[8] Boyle encounters another vessel named *Sally* but it is not known if it is the same vessel.

Overview of Atlantic Naval Operations in the War of 1812

The War of 1812 was fought between the United States of America and Great Britain and its colonies, Upper and Lower Canada and Nova Scotia, from 1812 to 1815, on land and sea. The United States declared war on Britain on June 18, 1812, for several reasons, including outrage at the impressment of thousands of American sailors and British restraints on neutral trade.

The Royal Navy lost early single-ship battles, but eventually their numbers became overwhelming and the naval blockade of the eastern seaboard began to hamper American commerce, with a major impact on New England interests.

The naval war was fought with the following U.S. vessels: six frigates and fourteen other vessels, and British vessels: eleven ships of the line, thirty-four frigates and fifty-two other vessels.

In the Atlantic theater, Britain, the world's major naval power, had recently gained a victory over the French and Spanish at the Battle of Trafalgar in 1805. In 1812, the Royal Navy had ninety-seven vessels in American waters. Of these, eleven were large ships of the line and thirty-four were smaller frigates. The United States Navy, not yet twenty years old, had only twenty-two commissioned vessels, the largest being frigates. Some were large, having forty-four guns, and were heavily built as compared to the usual British thirty-eight-gun frigates.

The strategy of the British was to protect their own merchant shipping with convoys to and from Halifax and Canada, and to enforce a blockade of major American ports to restrict American trade. Because of their smaller numbers, Americans sought to cause disruption through hit-and-run tactics, such as the capture of prizes and engaging Royal Navy vessels under only favorable circumstances.

In all the actions mentioned above, Americans had the advantage of greater size and heavier guns. American sloops and brigs also won several decisive victories over Royal Navy vessels of equal strength. In most of these actions, British gunnery and ship-handling was inferior to the Americans. American privateer gun crews were drilled for accuracy, whereas British crews sought to defeat the enemy by volume or rate of fire. While American ships had experienced, well-drilled volunteer crews, the best of the overstretched Royal Navy was serving elsewhere, and constant sea duties of those serving on North American stations limited their training and exercises.

The blockade of American ports had increased the number of American merchant ships confined to port. In addition to blockade, the Admiralty instituted a policy of permitting British ships to engage their American counterparts only if in squadron strength or by ship of the line.

NOTICE

TO PERSONS EMPLOYED ON BOARD PRIVATE ARMED VESSELS

To enable those who may be wounded, or disabled, in any engagement with the enemy, to obtain certificates entitling them to pensions, the like regulations and restrictions as are used in relation to the navy of the United States, are to be observed, to wit:

That the commanding officer of every vessel having a commission, or letters of marque and reprisal, cause to be given to any officer, or seaman, who during his cruise, shall have been wounded, or disabled, as afore said, a certificate of the Surgeon on board, to be approved and signed by such commanding officer, describing the nature and degree, as far as practicable, of such wound, or disability, naming his place of residence and the rate of wages, if any, to which he was entitled at the time of receiving such wound, or disability, and that such certificate be transmitted to this department.

The widows (or orphans where the wife is dead) of those persons who may be slain, in any engagement with the enemy, on board such vessels, will be entitled to pension certificates, upon forwarding to this office a certificate from the commanding officer of the vessel to which such persons were attached, of their having been slain as aforesaid; and the certificate of a justice of the peace, for the county in which such widows, or orphans, may reside, that they actually stand in that relation to the deceased.

Navy Department
Washington June 5 (1813)[1]

FOR THE PRIVATE ARMED VESSELS
OF THE UNITED STATES

***STRICTLY* confidental-.** *The commanders of private armed vessels are to keep this paper connected with a piece of lead, or other weight, and to throw the whole overboard before they shall strike their flag—That they may sink, and not fall into the hands of the enemy. For this purpose a cover of sheet lead will be the most convenient.[2] And such commanders are not to allow any person whatever, excepting one confidential officer, ever to see, or have a copy of this paper or to be in any manner appraised of its contents, on pain of forfeiting their commissions, and incurring all the penalties of law.*

That our public and our private armed vessels may be able to know each other at sea, the following signals are established: on falling in with each other the private armed vessel will hoist two flags, one above the other, and fire two guns to <u>leeward</u>, viz: [red] [blue]

The public ship of war will answer by hoisting any two of her flags one above the other, firing one gun to <u>windward</u>.

The private armed vessel will then haul down the two flags first displayed, and hoist one flag on the <u>mainmast</u> viz. [white]

The public ship of war will answer by hauling down the two flags first displayed, and hoisting one flag on the mainmast viz. on hoisting this flag she will cease to give chase, and the private armed vessel will immediately join her unless the public ship proved their hoist a white flag; in which case the private vessel will be at liberty to pursue her course. By command of the President (James Madison)
Secretary of State (James Monroe)[3]

Cruises of the *Comet*

The celestial comet of 1811 was the first great comet of the nineteenth century. It was independently discovered by Pierre-Giulles-Antoine Honore Flaugergues (1755-1840), of Viviers, France and by the young American astronomer and instrument maker William Cranch Bond (1789-1859), of Boston. The comet was visible in the northern skies throughout the night during the autumn of 1811. Because of its unusual brightness, the comet was widely observed in America and Europe. Few other comets have been one-tenth as bright, and only two comets with longer tails have been recorded. The comet attained notoriety, when Napoleon expecting the imminent outbreak of war between Britain and America, declared the comet a good omen for his ill-fated campaign against Russia. The comet is the one commented on by Pierre in Tolstoys's *War and Peace*.[4]

Fred W. Hopkins, Jr. indicates that a schooner privateer was launched in 1810 from Fells Point yard of Thomas Kemp. It is likely this vessel was named after such a heavenly visitor. Toni Ahrens in, *Design Makes a Difference in Baltimore, 1795-1835*, states the vessel was built privateer fashion: a round tuck schooner having a keel length of 68.00 feet, breadth of beam of 23.00 feet, hold depth of 10.00 feet and a weight of 164.60 tons, being built for Capt. Thorndike Chase.

Three cruises of the *Comet* are detailed in an article entitled "The *Comet* Harasses the British," published in *Maryland Historical Magazine*.[5] The source documents are a logbook, *Niles' Weekly Register* (a Baltimore-based national news magazine), and a contemporary newspaper account. The logbook is thought to have been kept by Dr. James B. Stansbury, the *Comet's* surgeon, who accompanied Boyle in the first voyage. Information on the third voyage comes from an article appearing in the *Baltimore Patriot* of April 4, 1814, wherein Boyle describes the third voyage.

1811
Background

Setting the stage of early nineteenth-century America, several events are worthy of note. In 1811-12, a major earthquake centered on New Madrid, Missouri, rocked the Ohio-Mississippi valleys. Tremors were felt over an area of 300,000 square miles. Major rivers flowed upstream and then changed their courses due to surface displacement of thirty feet or more (December 16–February 7).

Historian Richard Morris writes in the *Encyclopedia of American History*: "In May (16th), British cruisers off New York Harbor resumed more freely their impressment of American seamen. The British 38-gun frigate *Guerriere* overhauled (May 1) off Sandy Hook the American brig *Spitfire* and impressed a native-born American. Captain John Rogers, commanding the U.S. 44-gun frigate *President*, was ordered (May 6) to cruise off Sandy Hook to give protection to American vessels. En route Rogers sighted a ship he mistook for the *Guerriere* (actually the craft was the British 20-gun corvette *Little Belt*). Rogers gave chase; the *Little Belt* refused to identify herself; and the pursuit ended in an evening engagement (May 16) off Cape Charles. The broadside of the *President* disabled the *Little Belt*, killing 9 and wounding 23 of her crew. On November 1 the U.S. Government informed the British minister, Augustus John Foster, that it was willing to settle the matter amicably, provided Orders in Council were revoked."

Construction begins (1811) at Pittsburgh of side-wheeler *New Orleans*, first steamboat used on western waters. On maiden voyage she was caught in New Madrid earthquake, arriving at New Orleans on January 12, 1812.

The National Road is in various stages of completion. It is planned to connect Cumberland, Maryland, with Vandalia, Illinois. When complete, it becomes an important route of expansion and settlement of the West.

1812
Background

Congress declares war on Great Britain. Canadians, allies of British, defeat U.S. forces at Detroit. Northwest Indians under Tecumseh join the British war effort.

In Europe, the British under Wellington defeat the French at Salamanca, Spain and enter Madrid. Napoleon's Grand Army of 500,000 men invades Russia. Facing a severe winter, the Russians retreat and abandon Moscow. Moscow is set afire by the Russians after Napoleon enters city; over 30,000 structures are destroyed from September 15–19. Lacking shelter and supplies, Napoleon retreats with great losses due to winter, hunger, cold and Cossack attack.

English inventor John Blenkinshop designs and builds the first practical locomotive, using a tooth-rack railway.

Richard Morris in the *Encyclopedia of American History* highlights the significant actions at sea: "The skill and valor of U.S. seamanship were demonstrated in the engagement (19 Aug) off Nova Scotia between the US 44-gun frigate *Constitution*, Capt. Isaac Hull commanding, and the British 38-gun frigate *Guerriere*. After a duel lasting about a half hour, the *Guerriere* was so badly riddled and disabled that Hull had to abandon taking her as a prize and instead blow her up. The U.S. casualties numbered 14; the British, 79. News of the victory, coming hard upon reports of the fall of Detroit, helped to bolster sagging morale. The 18-gun sloop-of-war *Wasp*, Capt. Jacob Jones commanding, bested the British 18-gun brig *Frolic* in an encounter (17 Oct) 600 mi. off the Virginia coast. The U.S. losses, 10 killed or wounded; British, c.90. The 44-gun frigate *United States*, Capt. Stephen Decatur commanding, subdued (25 Oct.) the British 38-gun frigate *Macedonian* off the Madeira Islands and brought her into New London as a prize. The *Constitution*, under her new commander Capt. William Bainbridge, destroyed (29 Dec.) the British 38-gun frigate *Java* in a duel off the coast of Brazil (American loss, 12 killed, 22 wounded; British loss, 48 dead, 102 wounded). Her performance on this occasion earned for the *Constitution* the sobriquet *Old Ironsides*."

Louisiana admitted to the Union; Missouri Territory created.

Benjamin Rush publishes in Philadelphia his pioneering work on mental disorders called: *Diseases of the Mind*. He is subsequently called the Father of American Psychiatry. He was a Presbyterian doctor and signer of Declaration of Independence.

Log of the *Comet*

FIRST VOYAGE

(July 1812–November 1812)

[Logbook thought to have been kept by
Dr. James B. Stansbury, surgeon of the *Comet*]

On board the Privateer Schooner *Comet* of Balto. July 12, 1812, below Fort McHenry. At 3 P.M. got underway with several Baltimore. Privateer Schooners.

July 15. At 1:21 A.M. left Cape Henry all in good health and Spirits for a Three Months Cruise. Wind S & S.E.

July 17. Boarded Brig *Lamprey* Prize to the United States Frigate *Essex*.[6]

June 21, 1812. Three days after declaration of war 2 squadrons departed NYC including US ships *President, Hornet, United States* and *Congress* and brig *Argus*. Two days later *President* and *Hornet* gave chase to British frigate HMS *Belvidera* that escaped to Halifax. American vessels returned to Boston by August 31.

July 22. Boarded Ship *Active* of Philadelphia from Lisbon. Same day, Portugee Schr. *St. Franciscus*.

July 26. Lat. 28, Long. 59.10. At half past meridian on a wind standing to N. & E. to get the wind of a Ship then in sight on the same Tack. At 1 P.M. Tacked Ship to the South'd. At half past 2 P.M. could not weather the ship. Tacked the Ship to the Eastward. At 3 P.M. tacked to the South'd, Ship bearing S.W. by S. At 20 Minutes past 3 abreast of the Ship about a quarter of a Mile distant & She hoisted English Colours. Reef'd Foresail & put the schooner under fighting sail. All hands to quarters & Immediately bore down upon him. At 25 minutes past 3 P.M. he fired the first Shot which passed over us when a general engagement took place which lasted till 37 Minutes past 3 when down came the long boasted pride of Old to a Yankee *Comet*, without doing us any damage except a few grape Shot through our Sails & several which lodged in the waist. Ceased firing and on boarding found her to be the ship *Henry of Hull* near Four Hundred Tons burthen, commanded by James Dryden from St. Croix[7] bound to London. Her crew 20 in number, her metal 4 Twelve's & Six- Six pounders. Cargo per bills of lading 83 Hoggsheads 6 Tierces, 70 Barrels of Sugar, 19,160 lbs. Fustic, 3640 lbs. lignum vita, 13 pipes Madeira Wine. Finding her to be a lawful prize, took on board the *Comet* the first and second officer, & Thirteen seamen, sent on board the ship Seth Long as prize master. Edward Carey Masters Mate and nine seamen. Permitted Captn. Dryden & four Boys to remain in the Prize.

Augt. 4. Brig *Madaira* of Portsmouth N.H. from Cape D. Verds [Verde][8] bound Home. Lat. 28.57 Long.: [blank in the original] At 8 A.M. made a sail bearing S.S.E. Standing to the North'd. At 11 Tacked Ship to the Windward of the vessel about one mile distance. She appeared to be a large Ship. Bore away & run upon her and prepared for action. At 20 Minutes after 12 within Three Hundred yards of her, she hoisted English Colours. Fired a shot at us and prepared for action, when a general engagement commenced which continued very warm. At 35 minutes past meridian our fore topsail braces shot away, attempted several times to board the ship but was prevented from the masterly manner which she was maneuvered. Kept up a continual firing broadside after broadside and at intervals, a peal of musquetry from the marines. Ship makes a more feeble resistance. At 40 minutes past 1 P.M. she struck her colours to the *Comet* after being cut all to pieces scarcely a rope being entire. Mr. William Cathell and a marine Thomas Cadle the only persons on board wounded, the former very severely in the arm & leg &c from the blowing up of his powder horn while in the act of priming his gun (which hung fire so long he was of opinion she would not go off) the latter from a musket ball in the corner of the left eye. The *Comet* has not rec'd any very material damage except one grape shot which passed between wind and water, and a few lodged in the Hull & a number through the sails. Boarded the ship found one man dead, the Carpenter, and seven wounded amongst the latter: the captn. or Master, some of them very dangerous. On boarding she proved to be the ship *Hopewell* of London frm Surinam[9] for London, C.J. Lye Commander, William Anderson Master. She mounted Six Eighteens & Eight Sixes (Carronades) and Twenty five men including officers. Three Hundred & forty-six Tons burthen.

Cargo as per bills of lading 710 Hogsheads of Sugar, 54 ditto Molasses, 111 Bales of Cotton, 34 casks of coffee, 150 Bags Ditto, 74 bags of Cocoa. Permitted Wm. Anderson (master), two Boys & Three wounded seamen to remain in the Prize Ship. Sent on board the *Hopewell* John Hooper Prize Master & Eleven Seamen & ordered her for the United States.

August 19. USS *Constitution* sails from Chesapeake to Nova Scotia and captures and burns British frigate HMS *Guerriere* after 35 minute battle. Aboard the *Constitution,* is Lucy Brenner, serving under the name of Nicholas Baker as a member of the crew. She serves for 3 years, successfully disguising her sex.

August 24. Boarded Ship *Comet*[10] of New Port, R.I. from St. Ubes.[11] Put on board C.J. Lye Commander & Supercargo of the English Ship *Hopewell.*

August 26 Spoke Privateer Schr. *Swordfish* of Glouster[12] on a Cruise who the day before fell in with Two English Merchant Ships engaged them after exchanging a few Broad Sides had one man killed & one wounded. Sheired off. The *Comet* immediately went in pursuit of them but could not come athwart them.

Sept. 2. Lat 38.30. Long: 48.30. At 6 A.M. Discovered a sail standing in the Northern quarter. It was being at half past 8, a light breeze from the Southward. Set all sail could pack and immediately gave chase. At meridian discovered she was a Brig Standing to the Eastward under a press of sail. At 3 P.M. she hoisted English Colours. We prepared for action immediately. Gave him a gun & run up the American flag At 10 Minutes past 3 P.M. within Pistol shot of him to windward. Gave him part of Broadside. With a few shot from the musquetry, and down came the English flag. Not a gun being fired from the Brig. On boarding found her to be the Brig *Industry* of London from Surinam bound to London. Peter Holden Master. Mounting Ten Guns—Nines & Sixes. Thirteen men on board including officers. One Hundred and Seventy-five Ton burthen. Cargo as per bills of Lading[13] 195 Hogsheads of Sugar, 50 Hogshead Molasses, 32 Bales of Cotton, 10 Casks Coffee, 184 Bags of Coffee, 100 Ditto Cocoa, 8 Pipes Old Madaira Wine, 2 Hogsheads ditto.[14] Took on board the first officer & seven seamen. Permitted the Captn. & four boys to remain in the Prize, one of which had his Thigh Bone fractured & otherwise considerable Injured from a fall from the Top-gallant yard this morning inst. before they discovered the *Comet* in chase. Sent on board Solomon McCombs Prize Master[15] & Six seamen to navigate her to the United States.

Sept. 14. Boarded Schr. *Resolution,* Linzee Master from Boston bound to Cadiz.[16]

Sept. 16. Brig *Nancy & Kate,* Oliver Master from Philadelphia bound to Lisbon.[17]

Sept. 18. Lat. 33.00 Long: 57.00. At 2 P.M. discovered a Sail to the S. W. Standing to the N. West. a heavy squall came over at that time. However, made all the sail we could in Chase. At half past 2 P.M. tacked ship to the windward of the Chase which appeared to be a large armed ship. Bore away & run down upon her. At 3 P.M. hauled upon a wind again to Completely reconnoiter and made every preparation for action. Set the Fore topsail, reef'd and bore down again under fighting sail. At 20 Minutes past 3 she fired a shot at us & hoisted English Colours. Had six courses brailed up & appeared ready for action. At 45 Minutes past 3 he gave us three Cheers, we bearing down upon his weather quarter. At nearly the same time within musket shot. Bore away athwart his stern and commenced firing upon us from the great guns & musketry. At 55 minutes past 3 P.M. down came King George's Ensign, he having fired only Two guns into us, out boat and boarded her. She proved to be the Ship *John* of Liverpool mounting Fourteen Guns Twelve & Sixes, and Thirty one men, burthen 364 Tons. Cargo as per Bills of Lading, 223 Hogsheads Sugar, 3 Barrells ditto, 105 puncheons of Rum, 742 Bales of Cotton, 18 Tierces of Coffee, 35 Barrells ditto, 129 Bags ditto, 18 Pieces Hardwood[18] 3 Tierces Copper, 2 Boilers of ditto, 14 Pieces ditto. They had one man killed and several wounded. Ship very much cut in her sails and rigging. The *Comet* rec'd one shot in her foremast-which has dangerously wounded it.[19] Sent Purnel Austen Prize Master on Board with 12 Men to take her to U.S. Permitted the former Captn. four Passengers & Three boys to remain in the Prize. We then made all sail for the United States and arrived safe at Fort McHenry.[20]

October 6. Arrived at Fort McHenry after a pleasant Cruise of 83 Days, and had not a man killed during the cruise, and was never chased during the whole time. The owners of the *Comet* had determined to fit her out again with all possible expedition for a second cruise. The *Comet's* prizes have all arrived. The three Ships in this Port & the Brig in Beaufort, North Carolina.[21]

Author's notes:

Oct. 25. USS *United States* captures the British frigate HMS *Macedonian* and sails vessel to US port.

Nov. 9. Escape of HMS *Royal George* which was a 20-gun sloop operating on Lake Ontario. She was the largest war ship on the lake. On November 9 she was intercepted by an American fleet of seven ships but managed to escape to her home harbour of Kingston.

Dec. 26, Great Britain blockades Chesapeake Bay and Delaware Bay.

Dec. 29. USS *Constitution* destroys British frigate *Java* off Brazil, earning the nickname "Old Ironsides."

1813
Background

U.S. forces capture York (Toronto), and the British seize Fort Niagara and burn Buffalo, New York. The British begin a blockade of coastal ports and evacuate Detroit. Americans defeat the British at Battle of Thames, Ontario, in which Shawnee Indian Chief Tecumseh is killed, resulting in the collapse of the Northwest Indian Confederacy (an ally of British). Napoleon is victorious in four battles while allies defeat the French in five battles. The Methodist Missionary Society is founded.

Richard Morris in the *Encyclopedia of American History* provides more detail: "The blockade of Chesapeake and Delaware bays (announced 26 Dec. 1812) shut off commerce from those waters and was marked by British raids along the shores of the upper Chesapeake by a naval force under Rear Adm. Sir George Cockburn. The blockade was extended (26 May) to the mouth of the Mississippi and to the ports and harbors of New York, Charleston, Port Royal, and Savannah. Chesapeake Bay was used as a British naval station, and from the early months of 1813 until the end of the war the Southern coast down to Georgia was kept in a constant state of panic. After the announcement (16 Nov) of the blockade of Long Island Sound, only the ports along the New England coast northerly of New London remained open to neutral trade. The British hoped to exploit New England disaffection."

1 June. Destruction of the *Chesapeake*. The gloom that hung over the American cause in 1813 was darkened by news of the encounter between the U.S. 38-gun frigate *Chesapeake* and the British 38-gun frigate *Shannon*, 30 miles off Boston harbor. Acting against his better judgment, the commander of the *Chesapeake*, James Lawrence, accepted a challenge from Capt. P.B.V. Broke of the *Shannon*. Lawrence's sole advantage lay in the number of his crew (379) as against that of the *Shannon* (330)."

First successful sea voyage by steamboat *Phoenix* (NewYork to Philadelphia) designed by John Stevens.

Log of the *Comet*

SECOND VOYAGE

(November 1812–October 1813)

Private armed schooner *Comet* of Baltimore. Thomas Boyle Comdg. Sailed from Cape Henry[22] 24 Novr. bound on a cruise. On the 26th gave chase. Came up with & spoke the Schr. [left blank in the original] from Norfolk to St. Barts[23] Saint Barthelemy.

Boarded 3 Decr. Spanish schr. *Donna Maria*, from Halifax[24] to Havana.[25]

Decr. 9. (spoke) a Portuguese ship of 18 guns-from Pernambuco[26] to Oporto.[27]

Decr. 14. (spoke) a Spanish ship from Montevideo[28] to the Mediterranean.

Janry. 9. Made Pernambuco. Spoke a Coaster from Pernambuco, who informed us of some English vessels to sail in a few days from there.

Janry. 11. spoke Portuguese Brig *Wasa* from St. Michaels[29] to Pernambuco.

Janry. 12. At 1 P.M. discovered four vessels standing out of Pernambuco, laid by to give them an opportunity of getting off shore & to cut them off. At 3 P.M. they were upon a wind standing S.E. and about 6 leagues from the land. Bore up & made all sail in Chase. At 5 we were coming up with them very fast. At 6 discovered one to be a very large man of war Brig. Called all hands to quarters. Loaded the Guns with round and grape. Cleared the deck, and got all ready for action. At 7 P.M. close to the Chase. Hoisted the American Ensign & sheired close up to the Man of War Brig, who had hoisted Portuguese colors. He hailed & said he would send his boat on board. Accordingly, we hove too, and received his boat. The Officer said that the Brig was a Portuguese National vessel, mounting Twenty Thirty two pounders and one hundred and sixty five men, that the others were English vessels bound to

Europe, under his protection, and that I must not molest them. Captn. Boyle informed him he was an American Cruizer, and insisted upon his seeing his (Boyle's) authority to capture English vessels, which he did. He (Boyle) then informed him that he would capture those vessels if he could, that we were upon the high seas, the common highway of all nations,[30] that he had no right to protect them, that the high seas of right belonged to America as much as to any other power in the world, and that at all events (under those considerations) he was determined to exercise the authority he had, and capture those vessels if he could. The Portuguese officer observed he should be sorry if any thing disagreeable took place, that they were ordered to protect them and should do so. Captn. Boyle answered him that he should equally feel regret that any thing disagreeable should occur, that if it did, he would be the aggressor, as he did not intend to fire on him first. But that if he did attempt to oppose him or fire on us when trying to take those English vessels, we must try our respective strength as we were well prepared for such an event, and should not shrink from it. He (Portuguese officer) then informed us those vessels were armed and very strong. Captn. B. observed he valued their strength but little, and should very soon put it to the test. He (Portuguese officer) then went on board the Man of War Brig to communicate the conversation, with a promise of again returning. However, he did not. Finding he did not mean to return again, Captn. B. spoke the man of war immediately and asked him if he intended sending his boat back. He said he would speak his convoy, and request to send our boat on board. Captn. B. entertaining some suspicion of his motives for thus asking for our boat, told him he did not make a practice of sending his boat from the vessel after night, and should not do it now, and again told him his determination very distinctly, so that he should not misunderstand us. The English vessels were ahead of us, consisting of a ship of 14 Guns and 2 Brigs of 10 Guns each, making in all a force of 54 Guns. Made all sail immediately for them. Came up with the Ship (the three in fact were close together), hailed her & ordered them to back the main top sail.[31] He gave little or no answer, having quick way at the time shot ahead, but told him we should be alongside again in a few minutes, and if he did not obey the orders, we would pour a broadside onto him. After a few minutes (he) tacked. The man of war close after us. This was about half past 8

P.M. We then ran along side the ship, one of the Brigs being (near) to her, and opened a broadside upon them both. We were all carrying a Crowd of Canvas, and from superior sailing was frequently obliged to tack, and should have profitted much had the man of war not been so close, who now opened a heavy fire upon us with round & Grape, which we returned, having now the whole force to contend with. We Stuck as close as possible to the English vessels. They frequently separating to give the man of war a chance and we as frequently poured the whole broadsides into them and at time the man of war, who kept up a constant fire at us, when his guns would bear. About 11 P.M. the ship surrendered being all cut to pieces and rendered unmanageable. Directly after the Brig *Bowes*, our present prize surrendered. She was very much disabled also. We then proceeded to take possession of her, and as the boat was passing, the man of War gave us a broadside, and was very near sinking the boat, which was obliged to return. We then began again at the man of war, who sheired off to some distance. We followed a little and then made the third surrender, she being also cut to pieces. We was now again proceeding to take possession of the *Bowes*, when we again spoke the ship, the Capt. of which was ordered to follow us, who said his ship was in a sinking condition, having many shot holes between wind & water, and not a rope but was cut away. However he would for his own safety if possible follow us. At half past 1 A.M. took possession of the *Bowes* & manned her out. After this the man of war fired a broadside into her and passed her. The moon was not down and it became quite dark & squally, which caused us to separate, except the man of war, with whom we were frequently exchanging broadsides. At 2 A.M. he stood to the Southard, it being dark. We were out of sight of the other brig & ship which was in a southerly direction. We now thought it most prudent to take care of the prize till day light, the Captn. of which informed us the ship & other Brig were loaded with Wheat from Rio [de] Janario[32] bound to Europe, had sailed from there under the protection of this Portuguese Man of War Brig, and had put into Pernambuco for water, etc., and that the Captn. of the Ship before he struck informed him that he was in a sinking condition, cut all to pieces, and so was the other Brig. At day light we were close to the Prize. The man of war standing for us, we immediately hove about and stood for him or rather for the Brig & ship that was in the same direction. He tacked likewise, and shewed signals for Convoy to make the first port, knowing the Ship & Brig to be in a sinking condition & from the perishable nature of their cargoes which must inevitably be very much damaged. They being of little value and not in a situation to send to the United States I concluded not to take possession of them but to watch their maneuvers. They both bore up before the wind for the land I followed for some time, taking particular notice of them. It appeared at times to render them assistance. The ship was called the *George* of Liverpool[33] Captn. Wilson. The brig was called the *Gambier* of Hull[34] Captn. Smith.

At 10 A.M. went in pursuit of the *Bowes*, and at meridian spoke to her. I have since learned from several vessels which I boarded from Pernambuco, that the man of war brig was damaged very much. Amongst the wounded was the Captn. who had his thigh shot off & has since died of his wound, besides having her first Lieutenant [and] 25 men killed. The ships masts scarcely lasted to carry her into Pernambuco. Her cargo was nearly all damaged. She was dismantled & obliged to get new topsides put into her. The Brig was nearly in the same situation. The greater part of her cargo being damaged, and it was with difficulty they kept her from sinking before they reached Pernambuco Harbour.

January 17. Was chased by a Frigate & Schr. Could not make out what nation, after chasing about 4 Hours. Finding we beat them, they gave over the chase.

January 18. Land of Pernambuco in sight. Boarded a Portuguese Brig from the river of St. Franciscus to Pernambuco. Same day a Portuguese Ship from Lisbon to Pernambuco, and the Schr *Grand Sachem* from Philadelphia to Pernambuco, Gamble Master, out 41 days.

January 20. Spoke a large Portuguese Ship of 24 Guns (all Brass) from Lisbon, 44 days out for Pernambuco.

January 21. Boarded a Portuguese ship showing 40 guns (30 of them wood) from Lisbon to Pernambuco.

January 22. Spoke the Portuguese Sloop of War *Calipso* of 22 Guns.

January 23. Lat. 12.46 S. boarded a Portuguese Brig from St. Salvadore [Salvador][35] to Gibraltar.

January 24. Lat: 13.15 S. Gave chase to a Ship that proved to be a Two Decker Man of War, upon which discovery we made off.

January 26. In sight of St. Salvadore. Was chased by a 74,[36] a Sloop of War, a Man of War Brig and schooner. Crowded all sail, supposing them to be English, and escaped from them during the night.

January 29. At 5 A.M. discovered a sail to Leeward, standing to the Southard & Westward. Attacked Ship & made sail in pursuit of her. At 8 A.M. discovered her to be a tolerable large ship, coming up with the chase very perceivable. At 9 jibed the main boom over & set the lower Studding-sail, in fact, all the sail we could crowd. At 10 A.M. appeared to be gaining on the Chase, who had packed on a Crowd of Canvas to endeavor to get from us. At 11 A.M. coming up with her very fast she hoisted English colors. Still a crowd of canvas set before the wind. At 1/4 past meridian hoisted our colors, gave the Ship a bow Gun. Yawed off, & then whole broad Side, in hopes to cut away some of his rigging & disable him, as we sailed very fast, & to prevent a Chase too far to Leeward. Although we were long Gun shot off, in a few minutes we cut away his studding sail, halyards, &c and closed with him fast, when he began to engage us also. We now reserved our fire to close with him as quick as possible. At 30 minutes P.M. we were within long musket of him, and opened the broadside with the Great Guns and musketry at the same time upon him. At 40 minutes P.M. she struck her Colours, being much damaged in her sails & rigging, we having one man killed (John Dent) & two wounded, one with the loss of his leg. Board[ed] the ship immediately. She proved to be the Ship *Adelphi*, of Aberdeen[37] from Liverpool bound to Bahia Loaded with Salt & Dry Goods, mounting Eight Eighteen pounders, commanded by David Raitt. Sent on board Lieut. Cathel & a parcel of men to repair damages. Took out the prisoners. At the same time sent William Bartlett, Prize Master, and 11 Men on board her to take her to the United States. At 7 A.M. parted company with her.

February 5. Spoke a large Portuguese Ship of 16 Guns, 35 days from Rio [de] Janeiro, bound to Oporto.[38]

[At this point, Stansbury's journal is interrupted to insert this section from *Niles' Weekly Register*, not included in the original.]

February 6. On the 6th of Feb. at day light, discovered two brigs, to leeward, the island of St. Johns[39] bearing NNW, distant two leagues; made all sail in chase, and called all hands to quarters, discovered the nearest to be an armed brig; we coming up with her very fast; at 6, she hoisted English colors, fired a gun, and hauled them down again; took possession of her immediately; she proved to be the brig, *Alexis*, of Greenock[40] from Demerara[41] loaded with sugar, rum, cotton, and coffee[42] mounting 10 guns; sent Mr. Ball and six men on board to take her to the U. States, and made all possible sail after the other; at 8 A.M. discovered a man of war brig, upon a wind standing to the S.E. apparently from St. Thomas[43] found out by the prisoners that they were part of a convoy of nine sail from Demerara, bound to St. Thomas; that the greater part of the convoy had got in that night; that the man of war brig then in sight was the same that conveyed them, she was called the *Swaggerer*, at 9 A.M. hoisted our colours and prepared to give the brig we were in chase of, a broadside, when she hoisted her colors and gave us her whole broadside of great guns, which we instantly returned, and down came her colors; after she had struck, they cut away her topsail; and jib, haulyards, &c, in addition to the damage we had done by our shot, which was very considerable; sent Mr. Cathell, 1st Lieutenant, and some men to make sail and repair the rigging as quick as possible; took out the most of the prisoners with the boat I had kept belonging to the *Alexis*, and sent Mr. Giplin, prize master, and seven men in the boat to relieve Mr. Cathell; the brig by this time had made sail, and I filled away with the *Comet*; the boat being at a little distance from us, ordered it alongside for the purpose of gaining the brig sooner, but unfortunately in getting along side they sunk the boat and she was lost; fortunately no one was drowned; the man of war by this time had gained much on us; I thought it impudent to make any delay, and ordered Mr. Cathell to make the best of his way through and between St. Johns and St. Thomas[44] as the only possible means of saving the brig from recapture, and in the meanwhile I would with the *Comet* keep close to the man of war brig to divert his attention till he could escape. The brig captured was called the *Dominica Packet* of Liverpool, from Demarara to St. Thomas; loaded with rum, sugar, cotton and coffee, mounting 10 guns; I accordingly hove about and lay by to give the man of war brig an opportunity to approach me which he did to within gun shot; I soon discovered we were very superior in sailing; of course I could perplex him as I pleased, by either approaching or running away from him, as the circumstances required; we kept him in play in this manner till meridian, when I found Mr. Cathell had got through the Passage, who I had ordered to steer to the north and I would endeavor, if possible, to fall in with him at meridian-made all sail upon the wind, for the purpose of going round St. John's[45] and out of the passage between Tortola and St. John's[46] the *Swaggerer* carrying all sail she could pack in chase of us; at 2 P.M. had dropped him full four miles to leeward; at the same time discovered a sail upon our weather bow, and shortly after could discover her to be a schooner coming before the wind; at 3 P.M. was close to her; fired several muskets at her, and she hove to; put Mr. Wild, prize master, and six men on board, took out the prisoners, and ordered him through the passage between Tortola and St. John's; she was the schooner *James*, from Demarara to St. Thomas, loaded with rum, sugar, and coffee, the man of war brig carrying everything in chase though far to leeward.

[The following is Stansbury's narrative once more resumed.]

February 7. Boarded the Brig [left blank] (Portuguese) One day from Pernambuco to Angola.[47]

February 12. Anchored at the Island of Fernando [de] Norohna[48] for the purpose of getting wood and water. The Privateer *Yankee*, of Bristol[49] left there two days before, the sea being very rough, and dangerous landing, and the weather looking very ugly. Got under way on the 13th without being able to wood or water.

February 14. Brot to and spoke a Portuguese Brig from Bahia to Gibraltar.[50] Had spoke an American Frigate[51] three days before.

February 28. To windward of St. Bartholomews.[52] Was chased by his B. M. Frigate *Surprise* for 6 Hours. Out sailed her with ease.

March 1. At 3 A.M. on the 1st of March, made the Island of St. Bartholomews (Island of St. Barthelemy), & at 5 A.M. came to anchor in the Harbour of St. Barts (St. Barthelemy). At 7 A.M. was ordered out by the Governor who refuses us the privilege of being supplied with either wood or water. Captn. Boyle represented to him we were fearful his Foremast was sprung in consequence of which he permitted us to anchor again for a few hours to examine it. Meanwhile we made arrangements to get off wood & water in the Night unobserved. At 4 P.M. got under weigh & stood out of the Harbour, the Governor refusing to let us stay longer. At 8 P.M. fired a shot at a small sloop & schooner privateers (English) that were within Gun shot of us to windward. They immediately stood in shore for shelter. At 8 P.M. ran into the mouth of St. Barts Harbour & made signals that would be known to the Americans there, and the boats began to come off with wood & water. We lying to or Tacking in the mouth of the Harbour, received a number of puncheons of water on deck, with some wood, which lumbered[53] us very much, and put the decks in perfect confusion. At 11 P.M. the[y] absolutely refused to bring us any more water. Several vessels had just before come out of the harbour and run to Leward, and I presumed must have been captured, as I heard several discharges of Musketry, after the boats refused to bring us any more water. The Captn. of the Brig *Newton* of Balto. took the remainder on his deck, and got under weigh, in company with an hermaphrodite Brig, and ran out of the harbour, being bound to Balto. and for the purpose of delivering me the water in the morning at sea, and requested me to protect him during the night which had been previously agreed upon, and which we intended doing. We all then bore up together the decks were very much lumbered with water casks and wood. I turned all hands too to start water & clear the deck. Got up thirty muskets and as many Cutlasses and a precaution to be ready in a moment if anything appeared. About 20 minutes after we bore away several muskets were fired at us from a vessel upon our starboard quarter, we being then under Jib & Topsail only, so as not to run from the vessels in Company, who could barely keep company with us under that sail, and thinking these muskets were fired from a very small privateer that we expected was dogging us. Took very little notice of them, till after a few minutes, we discovered it to be a large [British] Schr. Privateer called the *Louis* of St. Kitts.[54] Close on board of us, it must be observed it was tolerably dark. The guns were immediately cleared away and gave him a whole broadside, (well told) damaged him very much. He jibed ship immediately in confusion, not expecting such a reception I presume. Could observe his sails & rigging very much disordered, and hear a considerable noise on board. In fact, hear a great number of shot strike him. Captn. Boyle would have persuaded him, not wishing to protect the vessels with him & fearful of their being captured if he left them, determined not to follow him, so kept company with them the remaining part of the night.

March 2. At day light made Dog Keys[55] At 8 A.M. made Sombero (in the Anegada Channel or Passage; aka Sombrero Passage). At the same time a large Man of War Brig stretching from under it towards us, from which causes we were not able to get the remainder of our Wood & water from the *Newton* following as well as she could. At 9 A.M. a small sloop, supposed to be a tender to the Man of War Brig stood towards us from the windward of Sombero.[56] She tacked close to leeward of us, and stood on the same tack with us. Fearful that his intention was to cut off the *Newton* when opportunity offered, we had fallen considerably to Leward of our wake, gave him one of the long nines, and he bore up close of the Island, and then hauled his wind again. The two Brigs finding the man of war approach them fast, they bore up, and we saw them a long time together. Continues to dog them till meridian, when they all appeared to run to leward.

March 4. Nothing very material occurred till the 4th. At 4 P.M. discovered a Sloop close in with the N.W. end of St. Croix beating to windward. Make all possible sail in chase. At 5 P.M. made a Tack close into the shore. The sloop did also close into the breakers. Fired several Muskets at him. He immediately bore up. Out boat. Sent Lieut Cathel & 11 men Men well armed in her in case he hauled his wind, and the *Comet* bore up & commenced firing at him from the great Guns, in hopes by the boat or schr. to get possession of him. The sea being rough, & he close in with the breakers, would do but little execution with the guns. He escaped by running round the west end of the Island. She was a fine Bermuda built sloop loaded with sugar. Agreeable to the Information which we had received, gave up the chase, and hove to for the boat to come on board. Received the boat and proceeded round the west end of the Island (St. Croix) and to the Southward.

March 5. At 2 A.M. tacked ship. At day light made a sail directly to windward of us. Made all sail upon a wind in chase. At 6 A.M. discovered it to be a ship upon a wind, trying to weather the west-end of St. Croix. At 8 found we gained upon the chase, and discovered it to be an English merchantman armed. At half past 9 A.M. she tacked again & weathered the east end of the Island. We could not weather. Made several tacks, and weathered away. Crowded all sail, but the ship had got near the harbour of Base (Basse-Terre) end. At 11 A.M. gave up the Chase, the ship having received a pilot, and got within the reefs.

[Here Stansbury's logbook comes to an abrupt end. Boyle, meanwhile commenced his course to the northward and he arrived off Cape Henry on the night of March 17, 1813. Evading the blockade in a thick fog, he arrived off Cape Henry on the night of March 17; he arrived in Baltimore shortly thereafter. There now occurs a delay until fall during which interval Boyle served with U.S. Navy].

Author's notes:

The operations of American privateers were extensive and lasted until the end of the war and were partially affected by strict enforcement of the convoys of Royal Navy. Some were audacious cruisers, even into British home waters. An example was USS *Argus,* which was captured off St. David's Head in Wales by the heavily armed British brig HMS *Pelican.*

March 14. American frigate USS *Essex* sailed into the Pacific in an attempt to harass British shipping. British whaling ships carried letters of marque allowing them to go after American whalers. *Essex* was captured on March 28, 1814 off Valparaiso, Chile, by HMS *Phoebe* and HMS *Cherub.*

May 25. British blockade middle states and southern states.

June 1. Off Boston, the frigate USS *Chesapeake* was captured by British frigate HMS *Shannon.*

Fred W. Hopkins, Jr. writes of this period in Tom Boyle's career:

> During the spring and summer of 1813 Tom Boyle and the *Comet* became members of the regular United States Navy. The British fleet had successfully blockaded the Virginia Capes and had moved up the Bay using small craft to attack American shipping and to raid coastal settlements. At this

time the regular United States Navy did not have craft of appropriate size, speed, and maneuverability to challenge the British fleet. Prompted by Baltimore insurance underwriters and by Captain Charles Gordon, U.S.N., commanding the naval forces in the Bay, the Navy Department authorized Gordon to hire four privateers to protect trade in the Bay and to keep the citizens of Baltimore and the Bay area informed as to the movements of the enemy. In addition to the *Comet*, Gordon hired the *Wasp*, the *Revenge*, and the *Patapsco*. Gordon informed the Secretary of the Navy on April 23, 1813, that the *Comet* had recruited her crew. On May 4, the message was relayed to Washington that the *Comet* was ready for service. On May 5, 1813, Boyle was given a warrant as Sailing Master in the U.S. Navy to date from April 16, 1813. On May 13, Gordon reported that he was employing the *Comet* and the *Revenge* to move buoys. Captain Gordon noted on July 17 that the *Comet* and the *Revenge* were in the lower reaches of the Chesapeake observing the movements of the British fleet. On August 26, 1813, Gordon received orders from the Navy Department to cancel the contracts and return the privateers to their owners.

Log of the *Comet*

THIRD VOYAGE

(October 1813–March 1814)

Overview of regional war news and other events: Creek War ends with the Battle of Horseshoe Bend, Alabama; U.S. defeats British on Lake Champlain, halting invasion to south via Hudson River valley.

British win at Bladensburg, enabling capture of Washington followed by bombardment of Baltimore Harbor and Ft. McHenry.

Napoleon loses six battles, enabling allies to capture Paris forcing Napoleon into exile on island of Elba.

English mining interests build and test traction locomotive (Puffing Billy) that hauls mining wagons without tooth-rack system.

The third voyage of the *Comet*, documented in this newspaper story, illustrates the seafaring and fighting skills of Tom Boyle and his crew. This voyage is Boyle's third aboard the *Comet*; it begins October 20, 1813, and ends March 19, 1814, when Boyle turned the *Comet* over to his lieutenant, Clement Cathell in Wilmington, North Carolina.

* * *

> The following very interesting extracts from the journal of the privateer *Comet*, of this port, have been politely communicated by Capt. Boyle, her commander, to the Editors of the *Baltimore Patriot*, for publication. The enterprise, skill and courage, which mark this distinguished commander and his gallant crew, cannot but give the highest pleasure to every honest American, by this new exhibition of them. Capt. Boyle dates this letter from Newbern, N. Carolina,[57] March 23d, 1814, where it will be seen, he arrived on the 16th.
>
> *Balt. Pat.*[58]

Oct. 20. Sailed from Cape Henry on the morning of the 20th of Oct. after passing in the night, all the enemy's squadron, laying in the bay, bound on a cruize in company with the privateer *Revenge*, of Baltimore (commdr Job West). (The two Baltimore schooners cruised together for three days only sighting two Spanish ships. They parted company on Nov. 1 and Boyle headed for the Leeward Islands).

On the 31st of Oct. boarded the Spanish ship, *Preciosa,* from Cadiz to Havana.

Nov. 1, boarded the Spanish brig *Fernandez*, from Malaga[59] to Havana; the same morning parted company with the *Revenge*.

Nov. 2, boarded the Swedish brig *Lucetta* from Boston for St. Barts,

Nov. 3, to Windward of St. Barts boarded the Prussian ship *Dei Biene*, from Gottenburg to Havana; lost one man overboard that drowned.

On the 5th Nov. to the northward of Sombrera,[60] boarded the Spanish schooner *Nuestra Senor de Cormon*, from Teneriffe[61] to Havana.

On the 6th, chased a sail to the northward of Saba[62] which proved to be an English frigate, out sailed her with ease.

On the 9th Nov. at night, near the harbour of St. Thomas, took the English sloop *Experiment*, of Guadaloupe[63] in ballast and destroyed her.

Nov. 11, was chased to the north of St. Thomas' by a man of war brig, out sailed her.

Nov. 13, just off Sail Rock Passage[64] discovered the St. Thomas convoy[65] about sixty sail of large ships, under convoy of the *Marlborough* 74, *Venus* frigate, and three large men of war brigs. The frigate and brigs gave chase to me, and after two hours chasing, gave over chase; same day, sent on shore at Tortola[66] on parole, the captain and part of the crew of the *Experiment*, and went in chase of the convoy.

On the 14th, discovered the convoy, and was chased off by the frigate and brigs—kept in sight of the convoy, and regularly chased daily, till the 21st sometimes very disadvantageous to us, and very advantageous to them, but always succeeded in out-sailing them.

Nov. 21, lat. -, boarded the Swedish schooner *Carlescrona*, from St. Barts to Bath.[67]

Nov. 22, From the 22d to the 27th, was chased every day by the frigate and brigs of the convoy.

Nov. 27, The frigate in sight, took the English schooner *Messenger*, from St. Vincents[68] to St. Johns[69] loaded with rum and molasses; manned and ordered her for the United States.

Nov. 28 was again chased; same day, boarded the Russian ship *Hazard*, from Liverpool to Amelia Island.[70]

Nov. 30, was chased again, and so continued daily till the 2d Dec.

Dec. 2, when, finding it impossible for one single vessel to do any thing with the convoy they being so strongly guarded miles from them, I concluded to abandon the chasing of them any further.

On the 3d Dec. recaptured the schooner *Industry*, of New York, that had been captured by H.B.M. brig *Recruit*, proceeding from Charleston to New York, ordered her for a port in the U. States.

The *Comet* then proceeded cruizing away to the S.E. of Bermuda, progressing as far to the eastward, as the long. 33°. 00'. W and then southward and westward, as far as the coast of Surinam, where she arrived on the 28th Dec. The same day chased a brig into Surinam river, but could not succeed in getting her, she having got under cover of the battery there.

Dec. 29, to leeward of Surinam, took the English sloop *Little Cherub*, of Surinam, of small burthen, having only Plantains (bananas) in, took some of them out, gave up the sloop and paroled all of the prisoners I had on board, and sent them on shore to Surinam; same day, took the English brig *Hannah* of Bermuda, loaded with lumber; ransomed her.

Jan. 2, to leeward of Barbados took the English schooner *Jackman*, of Barbados; loaded with lumber and a few cases of wine; took out the wine.

Jan. 3, took to leeward of Martinique,[71] the English sloop *Industry* of St. Lucia,[72] in ballast; ransomed the *Jackman*, and put the crews of both vessels on board of her on parole, and sent her away; same day destroyed (burned) the *Industry*.

Jan. 4, took the English brig *Enterprise*, of St. Kitts, from Grenada, bound to Guadaloupe, having on board a few barrels of bread and some specie. Took out some of the bread, the specie[73] and several other small articles of the provision kind, and ransomed her. My reason for ransoming and not destroying this vessel, was because she had the yellow fever[74] on board. But I wish it made publicly known, that the commander of this English vessel is an American, named John Howe, a man, I believe, well known to be unfriendly to his native country, and not long from it—a native of the state of Connecticut, I understand, he is to all appearances a great scoundrel.

Jan. 6, took the English sloop *Mary*, of St. Kitts, loaded with plantation stores, &c manned her for the United States;—since floundered at sea.

Jan. 8, took his Britannic Majesty's schooner *Vigilant*, John Benson, commander, tender to Admiral Laforey, sent her for the U. States. Same day, I paroled, and sent to St. Barts, the crews of the *Vigilant* and *Mary*.

Jan 9, chased a brig all night and fired several shot at her—in the morning at day light within gun shot of her, fired again at her when she rounded to, hauled upon the wind and made all sail in chase of us. We then found her to be a man of war brig that had been trying to decoy us.—We exchanged several shot—out sailed her easy, and she bore up before the wind.

Jan. 11, per log, discovered a sail, made all necessary sail in chase. At 3 P.M. discovered her to be a ship, running before the wind, to appearance tolerably large, carrying a great crowd of sail. At. 6 P.M. coming up with the chase fast, called all hands to quarters and got all clear for action. Could discover yellow sides and ports, which I took to be false ports. At 7 P.M. the ship began to take in sail—she took in her skysails, royals, topgallant and lower studding sails. We took in sail also, and furled the square sail, going so directly before the wind, had not an opportunity of seeing his broadside distinctly. At half past (9 P.M.) luffed up and gave him one of our bow guns, which he immediately returned with his stern chasers. We then closed and in a few minutes the action begun, and was warmly contested on both sides—at 20 minutes before 10 P.M. we had all the running rigging, with the boom topinlift, shot away—was compelled to haul off to repair. At this time we had one killed and a number wounded. The ship had boarding nettings reaching nearly up to her tops.

In a very short time we had repaired the damages and recommenced close action again, within half pistol shot, when he again shot away the boom top-in-lift. I was compelled to work the main with the peak haulyards. Made several attempts to board him but was not able to effect it. We kept up a continual fire on both sides; I shot across his bows and raked him several times, within 20 yards of him, but his tremendous height prevented much execution. At half past 12, midnight, fresh breeze; he now attempted to run us down, and so far succeeded as to run his jibboom into our mainsail, a little below the gaff, and come with his bows against our stern, without doing any damage to our hull, though he tore our mainsail all to pieces, broke the main gaff, unshipped the main boom. In this situation we attempted to board him, but could not succeed, he having quick way, & her height so great our man could scarcely touch the bobstays from our taffrail; though notwithstanding we had several of our men almost on her bobstays. We shot several of his men who were on his bow-sprit and forecastle, and took two of their boarding pikes from them as they reached down at us. He appeared to have many men on his forecastle, and splinter nets from his mainmast aft; hauled off again to repair, and bend another mainsail. At 1 A.M. had completely repaired and commenced close action again, which lasted till 3 A.M. at which time we had our jib stay, main shrouds, boom topinlift and fore gaff haulyards shot away— his fire appeared considerably slackened, our braces, topsail halyards and maintop sail sheets were also shot away, and the schooner was rendered almost unmanageable, many of the breechings of the guns parted. I thought proper to haul off till daylight; began repairing but found we were much more cut than I expected. The ship was about 2 miles from us at daylight, could count 14 ports on one side distinctly, guns in most of them. I determined to refit completely before I would again renew the action. The Islands of St. Croix, St. Thomas, St. John and Tortola in sight and at every little distance, I found the ship running before the wind, would drive me close to the harbour of St. Thomas, before I could refit, and renew the action, and not being in a situation to stand a chase, should any man of war make their appearance, and from information I understood several were at St. Thomas, I very reluctantly abandoned the idea of again renewing the action.

We had three men killed and sixteen wounded, myself among the number, at the commencement of the action, (tho' slightly) Mr. Edward Black, prize master, Mr. John Baney, master's mate, and Thomas Selma, carpenter, were the 3 killed. Six men badly wounded, the master of marines amongst them, and 10 slightly wounded.

Jan 13, close in under Spanish Town, Virgin Gorda[75] sent the boat armed to cut out several small vessels laying there—we destroyed one at anchor, and brought out two under a brisk fire of musketry from the inhabitants on shore, that had collected in a body. Both vessels were in ballast—we burnt one (a la Chesapeake) and sunk the other.

On the 15th arrived at the port of St. Johns, Porto Rico[76] to repair & get wood, water and provisions—was very kindly received by the Governor and allowed every privilege of hospitality I could expect.

On the 23d Jan. sailed from Porto Rico.

On the 27th Jan. took the English sch'r *Venus* of St. Thomas, from Laguira[77] loaded with coffee, cotton and cocoa, sent her for the U. States; the same day closed under the Island of St. Croix, took the English sloop *General Spooner* of St. Croix; this vessel we took with our boat armed, closed to the shore, the crew having deserted her a little before our boat boarded her; ordered his vessel for the U. States.

January 26, was chased across Drake's Bay[78] close to the town of Spanish Town, (Virgin Gorda) by a large man of war brig, carrying 20 guns, out sailed her with ease, and at midnight same night ran back under Spanish Town and cut out a small sloop laying there.

January 29, we paroled the crew of the *Venus*, and sent them in the sloop to St. Thomas.

Feb. 1, Gave chase to two in the evening.

Feb. 3, Next morning a very heavy gale of wind, kept sight of the chase, tho' far ahead of them and perhaps unseen by them, it blowing very heavy, too much so as to approach them with safety until the 3d in the morning, being to windward of them I bore down to reconnoitre, when I discovered them to be one a man-of-war brig convoying the other, that was a packet[79] —upon trial found I could outsail them, with ease, edged close down to them within gun shot, showed the American flag and gave them a gun, which each of them returned. We exchanged several shot and then departed. The man of war brig was called the *Wasp*. I then shaped my course southerly.

Feb. 6, off Saba fell in with the privateer *Mars* of New York, Capt. Jason Ingersoll. We cruized several days together in company and was chased twice very close but out sailed the chase. While in company we destroyed the sloop *Endeavour* of Anguilla[80] in ballast; parted company with them on the 12th.

Feb. 12, To the southward of St. Croix, he going to leeward for some repairs. He had taken one prize during his cruize.

On the 13th gave chase to a brig, at 8 P.M. that evening while in chase sprung[81] the foremast very badly, was compelled to abandoned the chase, take in all sail and endeavor to secure the mast in the best possible manner.

On the 16th February took the English sloop *General Wale* of Antiqua from St. Thomas to Laguira loaded with dry goods and manned the sloop for New Orleans.

On the 19th arrived at St. Johns, Porto Rico, where we were compelled to go refit & secure our mast—the evening before the *Pique* frigate[82] was off that harbour looking for the *Comet*.

On the 24th sailed from Porto Rico.

On the 28th of Feb. off Curacoa[83] bound to St. Thomas loaded with salt, cocoa, hides and goat skins, took out the cocoa and goat skins.

29th took the English sch'r *Enterprize* of Curacoa in ballast; ransomed the *St. John*, paroled the crews of both vessels and then sunk the *Enterprize*.

On the 5th March in the Mona Passage[84] was chased by a large man of war brig and out sailed her with ease.

On the 19th arrived at this place (New Bern, North Carolina) after a cruize of five months, and being chased during that time thirty-four times, by frigates and men of war brigs, but always out sailed them with ease. The Admiral on the leeward Island station, offered considerable reward for the *Comet*, as being the greatest plague to him of any vessel ever on those seas, but directed his smallest class of gun vessels and schooners to always run from her.

List of Prizes taken and destroyed during the *Comet*'s present cruise:

> Sloop *Experiment*, of Guadaloupe, in ballast, destroyed
> The Sch'r *Messenger* of St. Thomas sent to the U. States
> Sch'r *Industry* of N. York, recaptured sent to the U. States
> Sch'r *Little Cherub* of Surinam, sent with prisoners on parole.
> Brig *Hannah*, of Bermuda, ransomed.
> Sch'r *Jackman*, of Barbadoes, ransomed.
> Brig *Enterprize*, of St. Kitts, ransomed.
> Sloop *Mary*, of do. sent to United States.
> Sch'r *Vigilant,* tender to *Admiral Laforey*, sent to the U. States.
> Three sch'rs sunk, burnt and destroyed at Spanish Town.
> Sch'r *Venus*, of St. Thomas, sent to U. States.
> Sloop *Gen. Spooner*, of St. Croix, sent to U. States.
> Sloop *Endeavor*, Anguella, destroyed.
> Sloop *Gen. Wale*, Antigua, sent to New Orleans.
> Schooner *St. John*, of Curacoa, ransomed.
> Schooner *Enterprize*, of do. destroyed.

Making the whole TWENTY SAIL taken, burnt, destroyed and sent to the U. States.

THOMAS BOYLE, Captain

Overview

The campaign on the Atlantic Coast and the Chesapeake Bay

When the war began, the British naval forces could not blockade the entire U.S. coast as well as simultaneoulsy pursue American privateers. The British government, having need of American foodstuffs for its army in Spain, benefited from the willingness of the New Englanders to trade with them, so no blockade of New England was at first attempted. The Delaware River and Chesapeake Bay were declared in a state of blockade on December 26, 1812. This was extended to the coast south of Narragansett by November 1813 and to all the American coast on May 31, 1814. In the meantime, much illicit trade was carried on by collusive captures arranged between American traders and British officers. American ships were fraudulently transferred to neutral flags. The overpowering strength of the British Navy enabled it to occupy the Chesapeake and to attack and destroy numerous docks and harbors.

The strategic location of Chesapeake Bay near the nation's capital made it a prime target for the British. Starting in March 1813, a squadron under Rear Admiral George Cockburn started a blockade of the bay and raided towns along the bay from Norfolk, Virginia, to Havre de Grace, Maryland. On July 4, 1813, Joshua Barney convinced the Navy Department to build the Chesapeake Bay Flotilla, a squadron of twenty barges, to defend the Chesapeake. Launched in April 1814, the squadron was quickly cornered in the Patuxent River, and while successful in harassing the Royal Navy, it was powerless to stop the British campaign that ultimately led to the burning of Washington. After Washington burned, the British moved to capture Baltimore, a busy port and key base for American privateers. The British undertook a landing at North Point and were repulsed; then followed an attack by sea on September 13 but they were stopped by Fort McHenry at the mouth of the harbor. The defence inspired an American (Francis Scott Key) aboard a British ship to write the lyrics he called "The Star-Spangled Banner." In 1931 the lyrics became the national anthem of the United States.

During the blockade of the Chesapeake, the British had been instructed to encourage American slaves to defect to the Crown. Royal Marine units were raised from these escaped slaves on occupied Chesapeake islands, and they were trained to fight for the Crown. Some men and their dependents were taken to the naval base in Bermuda from which the blockade was carried out. There they were employed about the dockyard and a Marine unit was raised from among their number.

Naval History of Great Britain, by William James (1837), contains a chapter entitled "1813 Boat-Attacks, &c. in Chesapeake Bay," wherein he describes what the British were doing against the actions of American privateers:

> On the 11th of July Sir John Warren detached Rear-admiral Cockburn, with the *Scepter* 74, (into which ship he now shifted his flag,) the *Romulus, Fox,* and *Nemesis*, frigate armed en flute,[85] the *Conflict* gun-brig, and *Highflyer* and *Cockchafer* tenders, having on board the 103d regiment, of about 500 rank and file, and a small detachment of artillery, to Okracoke harbour[86] in the North-Carolina coast, for the purpose of putting an end to the commerce carried on from that port by means of inland navigation, and of destroying any vessels that might be found there. During the night of the 12th, the squadron arrived off Okracoke bar; which, accompanied by the *Conflict* and tenders, pulled in three divisions towards the shore. Owing to the great distance and heavy swell, the advance division, commanded by Lieutenant Westhal, first of the *Scepter*, did not reach the shoal-point of the harbour, behind which the large armed vessels were seen at anchor, until considerably after daylight: consequently, the enemy was fully prepared for resistance.
>
> The instant the British boats doubled the point, they were fired upon by the two vessels; but Lieutenant Westphal, under cover of some rockets[87] pulled directly for them, and had just got to the brig's bows, when her crew cut the cables and abandoned her. The schooner's colors were hauled down by her crew about the same time. The latter vessel proved to be the *Atlas* letter of marque, of Philadelphia, mounting 10 guns, and measuring 240 tons;

the *Anaconda* letter of marque, of New York, mounting 18 long 9-pounders, and measuring 387 tons. In the course of the morning the troops were landed, and took possession of Ocracoke and the town of Portsmouth[88] without the slightest opposition. The inhabitants behaved with civility, and their property, in consequence, was not molested. After remaining on shore for two days, Rear-Admiral Cockburn, with the troops and seamen, re-embarked without loss or molestation. Not, as it would appear, because he had performed the service in trusted to him, but, on account of his "not feeling himself competent to the attack on Newburn, not that its citizens were preparing to receive him." No sooner had the British soldiers and seamen departed, than the American militia flocked to the post; thus presenting us with a new system of military defense. Both the prizes were afterwards added to the British navy, the *Anaconda*, by her own name, as an 18-gun brig-sloop, and the *Atlas*, by the name of *St.-Lawrence*, as a 14 gun schooner.

On the 11th of July, at 9 A.M., the two United States' gun-vessels *Scorpion* and *Asp* got under way from the Yeocomico River[89] but soon afterwards were chased back by the British brig sloops *Contest*, Captain James Rattray, and *Mohawk*, Captain the Honourable Henry Dilkes Byng. The two brigs then came to anchor off the bar; and, seeing that one of her consorts, Captain Rattray dispatched in pursuit of her the cutter of each brig, under the orders of Lieutenant Roger Carley, assisted by Lieutenant William Hutchinson, and by midshipmen George Morey, _____ Bradford, and Caleb Evans Tozer.

Lieutenant Curry pushed up the narrow inlet of Yeocomico, and when about four miles from the entrance, found the American schooner, which was the *Asp*, of one long 18-pounder, two 18-pounder carronades and swivels, hauled up close to the beach, under the protection of a large body of militia. The British boats, however, persevered in their attack, and after a smart struggle, in which they had two men killed and Lieutenant Curry and five men wounded, carried the vessel. The American commanding officer, Lieutenant Segourtney was killed, and none out of his 25 in crew were either killed or wounded. The British set fire to the *Asp*, but not effectually as the Americans after-wards extinguished the flames and preserved the vessel.

Coggeshall writes (p. 79):

>
> Extract from the Log Book of the Schooner *Atlas*, Captain David Maffet
>
> August 3d, in latitude 37° 30', North, longitude 46° West, at half-past eight A.M., made two sail to the westward, standing to the Northeast; tacked to the southward; at half-past nine tacked to the northward; at ten A.M. beat to quarters and cleared for action.
>
> At half-past ten, bore away for both ships, and hoisted the American ensign and pendant[90] at three-quarters past ten the small ship fired a shot at us, both ships at this time having English Colors flying.
>
> At eleven A.M., the action commenced by a broadside and muskety from the *Atlas*, which continued with other ships at the same time) until noon, when the small ship struck her colors. We then directed the whole of our fire against the large ship, but to our utmost surprise, the small ship again opened her fire on us, although her colors were still down. We again commenced firing on her, and in a few minutes drove every man off her decks. At twenty minutes past meridian the large ship struck, and we immediately took possession of them both; one proved to the ship *Pursuit*, Captain Chivers, of London, of 450 tons, sixteen guns, eight and nine pounders, with a complement of thirty-five men; the other, the ship *Planter*, Captain Firth, of Bristol, of 280 tons, twelve guns, twenty pounders, and fifteen men; both with valuable cargoes of sugar, coffee, cotton and cocoa, thirty days out from Surinam, bound to London. We took out the prisoners, put a prize-master, mate and crew on board each of them, and steered to the southward in company. During the action we had two men killed and five wounded. Every one of

the shrouds on the larboard side were shot away, some of them in two or three places; the running rigging and sails very much cut. In consequence of the disabled condition of our rigging, and the fore-yard being gone, Captain Maffet determined on convoying the prizes to the first port in the United States to refit; kept in company with the prizes until Wednesday, the 2d of September, when at half-past four A.M., we made a large ship to the eastward, standing to the southward; at half-past five she tacked, and gave chase for us. We bore down, and spoke the *Pursuit*, and ordered the prize-master to tack to the southward, and make the first port he could. At six spoke the *Planter*, and informed him that the ship in chase was probably an enemy, and ordered him to make sail to the northward. At ten the *Pursuit* was out of sight to the southward. At eleven backed the main topsail, the strange sail coming up fast with the *Planter*. At meridian tacked to the southward. At half-past one P.M., the frigate fired five guns at the *Planter*, which obliged her to bring-to. Supposing her to be a British frigate, as she kept English colors flying, we made sail to the westward. At half-past three P.M., the frigate and the prize, *Planter* still in sight, lying-to, the *Planter* with American colors flying at the mizzen peak.

The frigate alluded to in this report must have been an American, as I find it subsequently stated that both these prizes had arrived at a port in the United States.

In *A History of American Privateers* (1899), Edgar Stanton Maclay writes (p. 251):

Captains Maffitt and Shaler

Two distinguished American privateers men who got to sea early in this war were David Maffitt and Nathaniel Shaler. The former, at the beginning of hostilities, commanded the *Atlas*, carrying twelve short 9-pounders and one long 9-pounder, with a complement of one hundred and four men. The *Atlas*, early in July, 1812, cleared the Capes of the Delaware, and when two days out she overhauled the brig *Tulip*, Captain Monk, just out from New York. The *Tulip* carried one of the British licenses referred to in the preceding chapter, and had on board one thousand four hundred barrels of flour and a quantity of salt beef. Suspecting that this cargo might be for the enemy, Maffitt pretended to be sailing under English colors, and kept up the delusion so well that the commander of the *Tulip* was satisfied that the *Atlas* was an English and not an American privateer. Acting on this belief, Captain Monk said that he ought not to be detained, as he had dispatched from "Mr. Foster," and then the commander of the *Tulip* showed his "British license."

"These papers," said Captain, "are quite satisfactory; and not, instead of sending you into a British port, I will send you into the port of Philadelphia." He then placed five men and a prize master aboard the *Tulip*, who carried the brig safely into that port. "We learn of a contract," said a Philadelphia newspaper of that day, "made at New York by Mr. Foster, and also one at Philadelphia, to supply the British armies [in Spain] with flour, etc., under British licenses, and we were in hopes that the ingenuity, enterprise, and management of our privateersmen would discover the traitors who were thus adhering to our enemies, giving them aid and comfort. Captain Maffitt deserves and will have the thanks of his fellow-citizens for the adroitness and judgment with which he captured the *Tulip*."

Continuing his cruise after his interception of the *Tulip*, Captain Maffitt, at half past eight o'clock on the morning of August 5th—or two weeks before the first frigate action of the war—discovered two sails to the west standing northeast, and he immediately tacked southward to reconnoiter. The *Atlas* at that time was in latitude 37°50' north and longitude 46° west. An hour later she tacked northward, and when satisfied he had merchantmen to deal with Captain Maffitt beat to quarters and cleared for action. At half past ten o'clock the *Atlas* bore away for both ships, and showing American colors, prepared to close with them.

Quarter of an hour later the smaller ship opened fire on the privateer and hoisted English colors, her example being followed a few minutes later by her consort. Maffitt, however, reserved his fire, as he was anxious to come to close quarters immediately. At eleven o'clock, having placed his vessel between the two English ships, he opened with a broadside from each battery, which was followed up with volleys of musketry. The effect of the privateer's cannon fire at such close quarters was terrific, and in an hour the smaller ship hauled her colors down. This enabled Captain Maffitt to devote his entire attention to the larger ship, which had been making a gallant fight and was keeping up a destructive fire. Scarcely had the *Atlas* turned from the smaller ship, however, when to the surprise of the Americans, the latter opened fire again, notwithstanding the fact that she had surrendered and her colors were down. Captain Maffitt reopened on his vessel, and in a few minutes drove every man below decks.

At this time a heavy fire had been kept up by the Americans from their opposite battery on the larger ship, and it was seen that he was suffering heavily. At twenty minutes past twelve her flag came down, upon which a prize crew was placed aboard her and her people disarmed. She was the *Pursuit*, a vessel of four hundred and fifty tons, carrying sixteen guns and a crew of thirty-five men. A prize crew also was sent abroad the second ship, the *Planter*. She was of two hundred and eighty tons burden, and carried twelve 12-pounders and a crew of fifteen men. Both ships were thirty days out from Surinam for London, laden with a cargo of coffee, cotton, cocoa, and six hundred hogsheads of sugar.

In this action the *Atlas* was badly cut up in her rigging and spars. Every one of her shrouds on the port side was carried away, which, with the loss of other standing rigging and the foreyard, placed her masts in a critical condition. Two of her crew had been killed and five were wounded. In view of the shattered condition of his vessel, Captain Maffitt determined to make for the first port in the United States and refit. Taking the crews of both the

Pursuit and the *Planter* aboard the *Atlas* for safer keeping, he headed southward, with his prizes in company. For nearly a month the three vessels continued on their voyage westward without molestation, but at half past four o'clock on the morning of September 2d a large ship was discovered to the east standing southward. An hour later it was seen that she was a frigate, and shortly afterward she tacked and gave chase to the three vessels. Believing her to be an Englishman, Captain Maffitt promptly bore down and directed the prize master of the *Pursuit* to tack southward and make the first port the could. The *Atlas* then ran close to the *Planter* and told her prize master that in all probability the frigate was an enemy, and ordered him to sail northward, Captain Maffitt deciding to take his chances with the frigate alone.

By ten o'clock the *Pursuit* was out of sight to the south; but instead of singling out the *Atlas*, as was expected, the frigate made for the *Planter*, and by eleven o'clock it was seen that she was fast coming up with her. Captain Maffitt now backed his main topsail and waited developments. At half past one o'clock the frigate opened on the *Planter* with her bow chaser, at the fifth shot obliged her to heave to. Observing that the frigate was flying English colors, and realizing that he could be of no possible assistance to his late prize, Captain Maffitt made sail westward. At half past three the ships were still in sight, the *Planter* flying American colors at the mizzen peak. As this display of the United States ensign on the *Planter* could easily have been resorted to by an English frigate as a ruse for decoying the privateer under her guns, Captain Maffitt kept on his course and gained port. Subsequently, he learned that the man-of-war was, in truth, an American, the 32-gun frigate *Essex*, Captain David Porter. Both of the *Atlas'* prizes arrived safely in port.

Refitting after her first successful cruise, the *Atlas* got to sea again; but Captain Maffitt, early in the summer of 1813, was compelled to run into Ocracoke Inlet, North Carolina, where he found the 18-gun privateer *Anaconda*,

Captain Nathaniel Shaler, of New York. Captain Shaler, like Captain Maffitt was one of the successful privateersmen of this struggle...

Early in July Captain Shaler ran into Ocracoke Inlet, where he found the *Atlas*, as we have seen.

On the night of July 12, 1813, Rear-Admiral Cockburn appeared off this inlet with the 74-gun ship of the line *Scepter*, the frigates *Romulus*, *Fox*, and *Nemesis*, the war brig *Conflict*, and the tenders *Highflyer* and *Cockchafer*, having on board about five hundred men of the One Hundred and third Regiment and a detachment of artillery, for the purpose of destroying these two privateers, which Cockburn had learned had taken refuge there. As this powerful squadron approached the inlet the masts of the *Atlas* and *Anaconda* were plainly seen, and the enemy at once made preparations for an attack. At 2 A.M. on the 13th the troops embarked in boats, and under the escort of the light-draft tenders and the *Conflict* made toward the shore in three divisions. Owing to the heavy ocean swell and the great distance at which the heavier vessels were obliged to anchor from the beach, the division under Lieutenant Westphal, of the *Scepter*, did not land until Daylight, which deprived the enemy of the advantages of night attack.

Having arranged their plan of attack, the British boats, under cover of a rapid discharge of rockets, doubled the point of land behind which the privateers were anchored, and dashed toward them in gallant style. Realizing that it would be madness to oppose the overwhelming force that was advancing upon them, Captain Shaler cut his cable and got ashore with his men, the British taking possession of the *Anaconda* without opposition. The guns of that vessel were not turned upon the *Atlas*, and Captain Maffitt, seeing the uselessness of resistance, surrendered. Elated with their easy capture of these formidable privateers, the enemy advanced against the village of Portsmouth, seizing that place, and were preparing to attack New Berne, when they learned that vigorous measures were being taken by the inhabitants to repel an assault. The project against New Berne was abandoned, and after holding Portsmouth two days, the enemy retired to their ships and sailed away. Both the *Atlas* and the *Anaconda* were taken into the British navy, the latter retaining her name and former rechristened *St. Lawrence*."

Chasseur Articles of Agreement

[This is a legal instrument where all aboard the vessel agree to the specifics of a proposed voyage in such matters as officers, shares, jobs, advances, etc.]

Articles of Agreement

Made and concluded upon this *Eighteen* day of *July* in the year of our Lord one thousand eight hundred and *fourteen,* between Captain *Thomas Boyle* commander of the private vessel of war, called the *Chasseur*, now lying in the Port of *New York* of the one part; and the Officers, Seaman, Mariners and others comprising the crew of the *Chasseur* of the other part, Witness:

That the said Captain for himself, and in behalf of the owners of the said *Chasseur* shall put on board of said vessel the necessary provisions, guns, powder, shot, and all other warlike ammunition necessary for the said vessel in her intended cruize; and that the net proceeds of all prizes that may be taken during the said cruize shall be divided *Three fifths* of which shall be taken for the account and belong to the owners, and the other *Two fifths* to be the property of the said vessel's company, to be divided in the proportions and according to the rates set against and affixed to the names hereto severally subscribed:

SECONDLY—That for preserving order and decorum on board the said private vessel of war, no man is to quit or go out of her on board of any other vessel, or vessels, or on shore, without leave obtained of the commanding officer on board, under the penalty of such punishment, as shall be esteemed proper by the captain and officers.

THIRDLY—That the captain shall have liberty to cruize where he shall think the most beneficial for the interest of the owners and the ship's company; unless he shall receive particular directions from the owners as to the place of cruizing.

FOURTHLY—That if any person be found a ringleader of mutiny, or causing a disturbance on board, refuse to obey the commands of the captain or officers, behave with cowardice, or get drunk in time of action, he or they shall forfeit his or their share, to be divided amongst the rest of the said ship's company; and be otherwise punished according to the law.

FIFTHLY—That such part of said Ship's Company, as shall be put on board of any prize or prizes that may be taken during the intended cruize, shall in all respects obey and perform the commands of the prize masters who may be appointed to take charge thereof, in the same manner as they are bound to obey the commands of the Captain and officers, while on board of the said Privateer; and in default thereof, the person or persons so offending, shall forfeit his or their share of prize money to be divided among the rest of the said ship's company; and be otherwise punished according to law.

SIXTHLY—That all articles found on board of prizes, that may be necessary and wanted for the use of the vessel or crew, to be taken by the captain without paying for the same.

SEVENTHLY—That is any person shall secrete, embezzle, or convert to his use, any part of the prize or prizes, or be found pilfering any money or goods, and be proved guilty thereof, he shall forfeit his share to the ship and company.

EIGHTHLY—That for the encouragement of merit, and to reward those who shall distinguish themselves by displays of courage and bravery during the intended cruize, there shall be reserved fourteen shares, to be appropriated by the captain and owners to those of the crew who, in the judgment, shall be most deserving thereof.

NINTHLY—That on the death of the Captain, the command do devolve on the next officer in rotation; and for the encouragement of the crew, on the loss of their Officers they are to be replaced out of the Ship Company according to their gallant behavior, as the Captain shall approve.

TENTHLY—That whoever deserts the *Chasseur* within the time of the cruize herein, shall forfeit this prize money to the Owner and Company, to enable them to procure others in their room.

ELEVENTHLY—All and every one on board do convenant and agree to serve on board the said Brig *Chasseur* for the term of *six months* effective at sea.

TWELTHLY—That if any of the Ship's Company shall be killed in the time of action, or in the Ship's Service, his representatives shall be entitled to receive his full share and proportion of prize money, of all Prizes that may be taken during the said Cruize, in the same manner as if he had survived till the expiration thereof.

THIRTEENTHLY—That all monies and other advances made by the Owners to any of the Crew before their departure from the port of New York be deducted out of their shares of the first prizes that may be made.

FOURTEENTHLY—That the owners of the said Privateer or such person as they or a majority of them shall name, be and are hereby constituted the agents of the officers and crew for receiving and obtaining from Clerks, Marshalls and other Officers of the Admiralty Courts, when the prizes may be adjudged all and every sum and sums of money that may be due and owing to them respectively, for and on account of their shares of any prize or prizes, which may be captured during the intended cruize; and for that purpose, shall have full power and authority to give the necessary acquaintances and discharges for the same.

AND LASTLY—Each and every of the said parties do bind themselves firmly to these presents to conform to and be governed by such regulations and orders, as may be prescribed by the present or any future laws of the United States, relatively to the conduct and government of Privateers.

IN WITNESS whereof, the said parties to these presents have hereunto severally set their names, and the day and year first above written.

Officers, Seamen, Mariners and others composing the crew:

Name	Station	Shares	Advance (dollars)
(Security agent: none listed)			
Thomas Boyle	Captain	16 shares	20
John Dieter	1st. Lieutenant	9 ditto	35
Thomas Coward	2nd ditto	8 ditto	35
Daniel Moran	3rd ditto	7 ditto	30
James Hamburg	Sargent Capt.	11 ditto	35
Isaac Webb	Master marines	6 ditto	35
Edwd Dew	Prize master	6 ditto	33
John B. Barker	"	6 ditto	30
Hamilton Stansbury	"	6 ditto	35
B. Chase	ditto	6 ditto	35
Abil S. Dungan	ditto	6 ditto	35
Cabil Coffin	ditto	6 ditto	35
Henry Pelham	ditto	6 ditto	30
not on board	ditto	6 ditto	
"	Surgeons mate	3 ditto	
Jacob X Burk	Carpenter	4 ditto	35
Alexander P. White	" mate	2 1/2 ditto	35
John X Jefferson	Boatswain	4 ditto	35
John Brown	" mate	2 1/2 ditto	41
E. Vinard	Gunner	4 ditto	35
Joseph Bullock	" mate	2 1/2 ditto	35
William H. Duvall	Masters mate	3 ditto	30
John Wheeler	ditto	3 ditto	30
A. Gantz Jr.	Quartermaster	2 1/2 ditto	35
Otho H. Davis	ditto	2 1/2 ditto	35
London X Williams	Sail maker	2 ditto	35
John Sutton	Armour	2 1/2 ditto	30
Hamilton Holsom	Ship steward	2 1/2 ditto	35
Joseph Gillit	Cabin steward	2 ditto	35
Daniel Adams	Seaman	2 ditto	35
John X Lennard	ditto	2 ditto	35
Joseph X Richardson	ditto	2 ditto	35
William Kelty	ditto	2 ditto	35
John X Barnes	ditto	2 ditto	35
John X Smith	ditto	2 ditto	35
John Rattiff	ditto	2 ditto	35
George X Walker	ditto	2 ditto	35
Thomas Weeks	ditto	2 ditto	35

Henry X Ratliff	ditto	2 ditto	35
Edwd Fitzgerald	ditto	2 ditto	35
Samuel Young	ditto	2 ditto	35
William X Harris	ditto	2 ditto	35
Hugh Duff	ditto	2 ditto	35
William C. White	ditto	2 ditto	35
John Frizill	ditto	2 ditto	35
Matthew Eldridge	ditto	2 ditto	35
John Ball	ditto	2 ditto	35
William X Smith	ditto	2 ditto	35
Joseph Rice	ditto	2 ditto	35
Charles Lewis	ditto	2 ditto	35
John X Nicholas	ditto	2 ditto	35
George X Roberts	ditto	2 ditto	35
John X Frederick	ditto	2 ditto	35
Kemp Southcomb	ditto	2 ditto	35
Samuel White	ditto	2 ditto	35
Lawrence Lutten	ditto	2 ditto	35
Edward X Crockner	ditto	2 ditto	25
Thomas X Saphy	ditto	2 ditto	35
John Hogan	ditto	2 ditto	35
George X Brown	ditto	2 ditto	30
Thomas X Di???	ditto	2 ditto	30
Daniel X Taber	ditto	2 ditto	30
Henry Wansor	ditto	2 ditto	30
Joseph X Gausaloa	ditto	2 ditto	30
Thomas Francis	ditto	2 ditto	30
Thomas X Graham	ditto	2 ditto	30
John H. X Brown	ditto	2 ditto	30
William Sommerset	ditto	2 ditto	30
Pierre A. Mason	ditto	2 ditto	30
W. Foster	ditto	2 ditto	30
William Suvs	ditto	2 ditto	30
Josse X Hollingsworth	ditto	2 ditto	30
Thomas X Davis	ditto	2 ditto	30
Obediah B. X Gould	ditto	2 ditto	30
Wm. Moroogon	ditto	2 ditto	30
John White	ditto	2 ditto	30
Francisco X Pedro	ditto	2 ditto	30
Peter Clark*	ditto	2 ditto	30
Henry Siming	ditto	2 ditto	30
Thomas E. Hammond	ditto	2 ditto	30
Barnard Duffie	ditto	2 ditto	30

John X Moran	cook	2 1/2 ditto	30
John X Berry	Bosn. mate	2 1/2 ditto	35
George X Moore	Ordy seaman	1 1/2 ditto	25
Benjamin Briggs	ditto	1 1/2 ditto	30
Thomas Smith	ditto	1 1/2 ditto	30
Thomas Cellis	ditto	1 1/2 ditto	30
Wm. X Jones	ditto	1 1/2 ditto	30
Nathaniel Patterson	ditto	1 1/2 ditto	30
John Bootman	ditto	1 1/2 ditto	30
Elijah Badger	ditto	1 1/2 ditto	30
Theodore Thompson	ditto	1 1/2 ditto	30
Benjamin X Brown	ditto	1 1/2 ditto	30
William Hogues	ditto	1 1/2 ditto	30
Richard Holmes	ditto	1 1/2 ditto	32
Robert D. Stansbury	ditto	1 1/2 ditto	30
Isaac Rhoads	ditto	1 1/2 ditto	20
Thomas N. Wake	ditto	1 1/2 ditto	25
Thomas Collins	ditto	1 1/2 ditto	25
Robert Weeks	ditto	1 1/2 ditto	25
Thomas X Rollinson	ditto	1 1/2 ditto	25
Henry Bettys	ditto	1 1/2 ditto	25
James Carpenter	ditto	1 1/2 ditto	25
William X Dickson	ditto	1 1/2 ditto	25
John Miller	ditto	1 1/2 ditto	25
Samuel Gibbs (Wm)	ditto	1 1/2 ditto	25
Jacob X Hill	ditto	1 1/2 ditto	25
John X Gleeson	Landsman	1 ditto	27
Samuel H. Sullivan	ditto	1 ditto	27
Francis X Dolphin	ditto	1 ditto	27
George X Farrill	ditto	1 ditto	27
John Whitney	ditto	1 ditto	27
Michael Reiter	ditto	1 ditto	25
Joseph S. Wiltberger	ditto	1 ditto	15
Thomas Liauter	ditto	1 ditto	15
Robert Caskey	ditto	1 ditto	15
Jacob X Perkins	ditto	1 ditto	15
Overton Addison	ditto	1 ditto	15
William X Henry	ditto	1 ditto	15
H. M. Dongall	ditto	1 ditto	15
Joseph Wilder	ditto	1 ditto	15
Edward Liscure	ditto	1 ditto	15
John X Pircy	boy	3/4 ditto	25
Abraham Hoppings	ditto	3/4 ditto	25

Adam Hurst	ditto	3/4 ditto	25
Philip X Low	ditto	3/4 ditto	25
Comet Chase	ditto	3/4 ditto	25
Yankee Sheppard	ditto	3/4 ditto	25
John X Frame	ditto	3/4 ditto	15
Ruben G. X Gordon	ditto	3/4 ditto	15
Thomas X Tyler	ditto	3/4 ditto	15

*In other documents Peter is identified as a black man who was wounded and died soon after the action. See *Niles' Weekly Register*, Saturday, March 23, 1815, No. 4 of Vol. VIII.

The list of crew uses the "X" symbol 44 times with the notation: "His X Mark"

Note: The transcription of the log reveals John McConkey was lost overboard from the ship on December 27, 1814, "by a wash of a sea." There is no reference to John McConkey in the list of men aboard in the ship's Articles. Possibly he was signed on in New York. The Articles account for two men who were documented but not on board, one being a surgeons mate. Perhaps McConkey was one of them.

JOURNAL OF PRIVATE ARMED BRIG *CHASSEUR*
Thos. Boyle, Commander
from New York on a cruise
December 1814–March 1815

Compiler's remarks:

"Chasseur," a French word, is included in *The American Heritage Dictionary of the English Language* with the following meanings: a soldier, especially one of certain light cavalry or infantry troops of the French army trained for rapid maneuvers, a huntsman or a uniformed footman. This French word is derived from Old French chaceour and chacier, meaning to chase.

The following is a composite log of "Thomas Boyle, Commander, from New York on a cruise," and is based on 1) the compiler's transcription of a copy of the handwritten log of *Chasseur* held by the Maryland Historical Society and 2) "Log of the *Chasseur*" printed in *Maryland Historical Magazine*, Volume I, 1906, pp. 168-180; 218-240.

Variances between logs: The compiler points out that his copy of log (dated 1814-1815) was imperfect, being a Xerox copy of the original. The 1906 copy was examined and transcribed 98 years ago and subject to more extensive examination by the staff of the *Maryland History Magazine* than was possible with the Xerox copy. In light of this, the compiler favored the 1906 version. On a copy of the 1814-1815 log the compiler marked all those words and phrases that he could not readily understand, being 84 in number. Usage of punctuation marks was minimal in the 1814-1815 copy. Additionally the sea detail register with each entry of the log did not exist for 21 days, being a description (every other hour) of ships speed in knots, fathoms from soundings, ship's course and wind direction encountered by the ship.

Examples of the variances between the logs include:

1) Punctuation: 1814-1815 version has minimal attention to punctuation (especially periods and commas). The 1814-1815 log uses the ampersand throughout while the 1906 version uses the word "and."

2) Sentence structure variation. In many instance the original log entry is abbreviated but in the 1906 entry it has been completed for ease of reading.

3) Ship descriptor (brig vs. brigantine). The only place the word brigantine is used is in the testimony of Dieter and Cathell, the last item of the log. Fred. W. Hopkins, Jr. in "Tom Boyle: Master Privateer" (p. 47) mentions that when rerigged in New York, the Chasseur became a brigantine. However, the handwritten heading on each page of the log indicates that the Chasseur was a brig.

4) Legibility:
The 1814—1815 log had 8 pages that were too faded to read (Feb 3-10, 1815)

5) Daily observations:
The 1814—1815 log has 82 entries. Of that number 21 of the daily conditions are missing, not observed or not recorded. These record for every other hour of day: ship speed in knots, fathoms of water, courses direction and direction of winds.

6) Missing pages:
The 1814—1815 log had 6 pages that were missing (Dec. 31 1814 to Jan. 1-5 1815).

7) Entry organization: 1906 log breaks down the entries into distinct paragraphs including "Commences" (beginning of day), "Meridian" (noon), "Midnight" and "Closes" (last entry for day). The 1814-1815 log runs this content together.

Overview of Events and Inventions of 1815

General Jackson defeats the British at Battle of New Orleans, fought two weeks after the signing of the Treaty of Ghent. The Anglo-American commercial treaty ends British duties against U.S. ships and vice versa. Napoleon returns to France for "Hundred Days." Wellington and Prussian forces defeat the French under Napolean at Battle of Waterloo and Napoleon is exiled to St. Helena. The Congress of Vienna is convened and readjusts many political boundaries of Europe. New England textile mills process 90,000 bales of cotton in one year, up from only 500 bales in 1800. Sir Humphry Davy invents the miner's safety oil lamp, saving many lives. Chief imports to U.S. are woolen and cotton items, sugar and coffee; the main export is raw cotton. In the opening of the West the Conestoga wagon is the prime mover, having a four to six horse team pulling a load of several tons and measuring 60 feet.

British inventor George Stephenson builds a locomotive he calls "Blucher" that can pull loads faster than a horse team.

The percussion cap is invented in the United States by Joshua Shaw, making possible breech-loading firearms that are easier to reload and which increases soldiers' firepower. The first steam-powered warship, called *Demologos Fulton,* is built in the U.S. Designed by Robert Fulton to carry 32 guns, it never sees action. The modern method of roadbuilding is developed by British engineer John McAdam, employing crushed rock of differing interlocking sizes.

[The log of the *Chasseur* begins in New York Harbor]

Remarks on board Friday December 23 1814
At 10 AM got underway from the North River[91] and stood down to Staten Island[92] and anchored at the Quarentine Ground[93] Sent the boat ashore for several loads of water[94] sent down the Fore Royal yard. At 2 PM Captain came on board; got underway, and stood down. At 4 PM sent the boat ashore to Fort Richmond[95] Got permission to pass at 6 PM passed Sandy Hook[96] End the Civil Day.

[While in New York Harbor, the *Chasseur* was rerigged from a top sail schooner to a brig having two masts with square sails on the fore and main masts. The main mast has a Driver or Spanker sail (fore and aft). She also got a new paint scheme of black with two yellow stripes along her sides.]

Sam Svensson, in *Sails Through The Centuries,* says:

> The brig rig was very popular for a long time because of its maneuverability. The advantage of a square sail is that it can be braced (to turn the yards of a ship by the braces; a rope by which a yard is swung and secured on a square-rigged ship; a rope rove through a block at the end of a ship's yard to swing it horizontally) in such a way that its front side catches the wind and thus the ship is taken aback or forward motion stopped or slowed. With her symmetrical rig, a brig could sail forward or backward, stand still in the water, or turn on the spot, all depending on how the sails were braced. In exotic ports where there were no tow boats, the brigs could manage through their own maneuvering better than other ships.

We read in the log that this capability was used frequently as the *Chasseur* was a fast sailer when in company of other ships needed to be taken aback occasionally to advantageously engage the opposing ship(s) as happened with convoys in the West Indies.

Henry B. Culver writes in *The Book of Old Ships*, "Brigs are very handy and many of them sail fast. They were a favorite medium of privateering, and it was a short step from that occupation to piracy. And the brig was what might have been termed the pirates' own vessel."

Hopkins, Jr. comments in his book, *Tom Boyle: Master Privateer*, that the *Chasseur* was rerigged in New York and went to sea as a brigantine, which is not consistent with the log entry titles which read "Journal of Private Armed Brig *Chasseur*."

If the spars were cut to proper size, the rerigging from schooner to brig could be easily effected as the masts were not changed nor were the shrouds or stays.]

Remarks on board Saturday 24th Decr.
At 7 PM the light bore W by N distance 3 leagues. At 8 the Highlands of Neversink[97] bore W by N distance 7 leagues from which we take our departure. All necessary sail set. Set the watch and clear'd up the decks.
Midnight stiff breezes and pleasant, tho' cold. At 4 PM took in the Studding Sails. at 5 AM in the Fore Top Gallant Sail at 6 AM set the Fore Sail. At 9 AM unbent the cables and stored, people employed at sundry jobs of Ships duty. At 11 AM fresh breeze. Handed fore top Gallant sail. Lat by Ob 38° 54 N

Remarks on board Sunday 25th Decr.
At 5 PM double reef the Main Sail, fore top, breezes.
Midnight cloudy. Jibbed over the Main boom. Wind from the Eastward At 6 set the Fore Top Gallant Sail. Meridian set the Jibbs and let the reefs out of the Main Sail. Lat. by Obn 36° 24 N.

Remarks on board Monday 26th Decr.
Commences with light Breezes and Cloudy. Heavy swell from the NW. At 5:30 AM reefed the Main Sail and took in the Jibb; at 7 double reefed the Fore Top Sail and single reefed the Main one. At 10 AM close reefed the Fore top sail and the Square Fore Sail. Balance reefed the Main Sail, and took two reefs in the Fore and Aft Fore Sail. At the same time sent down the Fore top Gall. yard. Fresh gales and squally. Lat. by indt. Obn 35° 18 N.

Remarks on board 27th Decr.
At Meridian wore Ship and stood to the Southward. Very squally disagreeable looking weather. At 4 PM sent down the Main yard and the Fore Top Gallant Mast and got in the Flying Jibb boom. At 5 PM heavy Sea carried away the Main boom. Lowered down the Main Sail and got the Boom on board to Fish it. Carpenter and crew employed in getting all ready to fish boom. At Midnight squally

from the Northward & Westward. At 2 AM heavy and severe Gales, the Decks full of Water carried away the Sprit Sail yard and Fore Gall, the Brig laboring very heavy and Shipping much Water. Lost John McConkey[98] overboard by the Wash of a Sea and never saw him more. At day light set up the Fore rigging and commenced putting the (ship) in order. At 8 AM set the Fore Top sail close reefed, Carpenter employed in securing the Wedges[99] of the Main Mast that had worked loose, and fishing the Main Boom. Much damaged done to our hull and Rigging. Employed in refitting. Decks constantly filled with water. Ends heavy Gales and Squally. Lat by Obn 33° 23 N.

Remarks on board Wednesday 28th Decr.
Commences fresh gales and squally. Carpenter & Crew employed in fishing the Main Boom. At 5 P.M. handed the Fore top sail and set the Fore and aft Foresail double reefed, at the same time hove her to, head to the S.W. At midnight winds moderate but frequently squally with fine rain. At 7 AM bore away and made sail. Carpenter as before employed in fishing the Main Boom. At 10 AM set the square foresail and Jibb. Let out the reefs of the Fore and Aft Foresail and loosed the Main Sail to dry. At Meridian swayed up the Fore top Gallant Mast and let out one reef of the Fore Top sail. Lat by Obn. 31° 59 North

Remarks on board Thursday 29th December
Commences with Steady Breezes and more pleasant Weather. Carpenter still employed in Fishing the Main Boom. All Sail set as necessary. Midnight pleasant Weather. At 8 AM got the Main boom shipped and sent up the Fore top Gallant yard. Fished the Sprit sail yard and otherwise employed in Sundry Jobs of ship's duty. Meridian pleasant Lat by obs. 30° 00 N

Remarks on board Friday 30th December
Commences with moderate winds and frequent squalls of fine Rain. Exercised the Great Guns and small Arms. The crew otherwise employed in Sundry Jobs of Ships Duty. All the necessary Sail Set. Midnight as before. Latter part employed in various Jobs of Ships Duty. The Gunner, Carpenter of Crew variously employed Lat by Obn. 28. 52 N.

Remarks on board Saturday 31st December
Begins with Cloudy obscured Weather and frequent squalls of fine Rain. Exercised great Guns[100] and small Arms. At 6 PM handed the Fore top Gallant Sail. At Midnight fine rain. Took two reefs in the Main Sail. Latter part pleasant. Boatswain, Carpenter and Gunners employed at Sundry Jobs of Ship's Duty. Sent up the fore Royal Mast and yard and Set all Sail necessary. Ends pleasant and Clear. Lat. Ob. 27. 09 North

Remarks on board Sunday 1st. January 1815
Commences with fine Breezes and pleasant Weather. All Necessary Sail set. At 4 PM exercised the Great Guns and Small arms with powder. Midnight pleasant. Wind inclines to the Northward. At 8 AM set Steering Sails below and aloft, and lowered the Main sail down. Ends pleasant. Lat ob. 24. 44 North

Remarks on board Monday 2d. January
Commences with fine Breezes and Clear pleasant Weather. At 4 PM exercised Great Guns and Small Arms. All necessary sail set. At 6 PM on Steering Sails[101] below and Aloft.
Midnight fresh Breezes and Pleasant. Took in the Main Top Gallant Sail and Fore Royal. At 8 AM took in Fore top Gallant Sail. At 10 AM lowered the sails down to set up the fore rigging. Employed at Ditto. Meridian rather squally. Made sail Lat ob. 21. 26 North

Remarks on board Tuesday 3d. January
Commences with fresh Breezes and flying Clouds. At 2 PM handed the Fore Top Gallant Sail At 4 single reefed Fore and Main Top Sail. At 6 took in the Jibb. At 4 single reefed Fore and Main Top Sail. At 6 took in the Jibb. Frequent little squalls of Rain
Midnight frequent little squalls of Rain. Lowered down the Main Sail frequently in the rain. At 7 AM set the Jibb. At 8 set the Fore top Gallant sail. Ship's Crew employed in Various Jobs of Ship duty. Discovered the Fore and Main Masts a little Sprung; presume nothing of consequence. Lat by ob. 17. 44 North

Remarks on board Wednesday 4th December (this should be Jan)
Commences with fresh Breezes and pleasant Weather. Employed at Sundry Jobs and Ship's duty and fishing in part the Main Mast. At 6 PM took in the Fore top Gallant Sail and Jibbs. Frequent little squalls of fine Rain. Midnight pleasant. Latter part employed in

rewoolding the fishes on the Main boom and other necessary Jobs. Lat Ob. 14. 14 North

Remarks on board Thursday 5th January
At 3 1/2 P.M. made the East end of Barbadoes bearing SSW, distant 8 leagues. At 6 P.M. north part bore SWS Distant 8 leagues. East end S.W. distant 9 leagues. At 8 PM hauled up the square Fore Sail and Jibbs and backed the Main Top Sail. At 7 AM kept away west. At 8 Made the land bearing NW. At 9 Made all Sail. SE part of the Island of Barbadoes bearing NW three leagues distant. Employed at Sundry Jobs of Ship's duty. Meridian. within 2 leagues of the land. Lat Obr 13. 03 North

Remarks on board Friday 6th January 1815
Commences with fine breezes and pleasant Weather. At 6 PM the South end of Barbados bore NW by W and the east end NNW 4 leagues distant. At Midnight tacked Ship to the northd. At 4 AM tacked Ship to the Southd. At 5 AM tacked again. At 7 AM. Barbadoes bore NW distant 7 leagues. At 9 discovered a Sail bearing North. Made all sail in chase. At 10 discovered her to be a Ship running before the Wind. At 11 She haul'd her Wind for us. We then plainly perceiving her to be a large Ship of War, tacked ship & made every preparation for Action. At 11 1/2 tacked Ship and passing her to windward hoisted the Yankee Flag and gave her one of our long 12 (pounder) which she returned with several Guns without doing us any injury. Meridian tacked again and passing her fired several Shot at her, which she returned. Some of her Shot over reached us.[102] Lat Ob 13- 03 North

Remarks on board Saturday 7th January 1815
At 1 PM the Sloop of War bore up. After having fired many Shot at her, we bore up also. A Man of War Brig in signal to Leeward. At 2 P.M. could see the Shipping in the harbour of Bridgetown[103] & the Admiral's Ship making signals to the one we had engaged and the Brig also. They both hauled upon a wind in chase of us, and a frigate came out of Bridgetown also in Chase. Stood close in Shore & took the Schooner *Elizabeth* of Bridgetown. Brought her alongside and took her in tow. Took out Several Articles & burnt her. The Three Men of War close by. Made all necessary sail on a Wind.

Midnight tacked Ship. At 5 AM tacked Ship. Discovered a Frigate or 74 close to us standing on the other tack. At 6, she hove about and gave us Chase. Beat her with ease. At 8 AM. gave over Chase. At 9 discovered Three Sails off the Weather bow. Directly after all three gave us Chase.

At Meridian we appeared to leave the Vessels fast whom we supposed to be the same that chased us yesterday, two Ships and a Brig, every possible set in chase of us. Employed in Sundry Jobs of Ship's duty. Latd. Ob 12. 16 North

Remarks on board Sunday 8th Jany 1815
Commences with stiff Breezes & pleasant Weather. At 2 PM observed the three Men of War in Chase of us making signals to each other, but we were leaving them fast. At 3 PM lost sight of one of them astern. At 7 PM bore up WSW & lost sight of them all.
Midnight fine Breezes. At daylight made Small Schooner to the windward. Made every necessary sail in Chase and they did the same to escape us.
Meridian Wind very light. A cross swell and we do not near the Chase in consequence of the lightness of the Wind.
Latd Ob. 11. 53 North.

[On this day the Battle of New Orleans was fought.]

Remarks on board Monday 9th January
Commences light Airs next to calms. Out sweeps[104] at 2 PM and continued them out till 6 without gaining on the Chase. At 8 tacked Ship. At 10 tacked ship.
Midnight squally. At 1 AM tacked Ship. At 2 heavy squalls. Took in sail. At 4 discovered the Main Mast badly sprung in the do place, much more than we expected. At Daylight commenced setting up the Main Rigging & getting the Mast ready for fishing.
Latter part employed in fishing the Mast to the best advantage, not having the means to do it effectually. End fresh Breezes & heavy sea. Lat. Obs 12 27 North

Remarks on board Tuesday 10th January 1815
Commences with fresh Gales and Heavy Seas. At 2 PM fished Main Mast, tho' not as we could wish. At 4 PM set the three-reefed Main sail. At 11 PM tacked Ship.

Midnight squally. At 3 AM tacked ship. At 6 made the Island of St Vincents[105] bearing NNW distant 3 leagues. At 9 AM saw a Sloop & Schooner standing to Windward from the west end of the Island. Endeavored to cut them off, but they took Shelter under a small Fort. At 11 AM sent the Boat and took possession of the Sloop *Eclipse* of St. Vincents from Grenada to St. Vincent, having on board a few Boxes of candles & two Cases Irish Linnens[106] Took out the linnens & Candles with the Prisoners and sank her.

Meridian clear & pleasant. Bore up in chase of a sail to Leeward, the principal harbour of St. Vincents bearing North 2 Leagues.

Remarks on Board Wednesday 11th January 1815
At 2 PM sent the Boat to cut off a Small Schooner to Leeward under English Colours, but a breeze springing up she escaped into the harbour of Bequia.[107] Ran to Leeward & made sail amongst the Grenadene Keys.[108] Gave chase. At 4 PM sent the Boat Armed. The Crew having deserted her, the Boat took possession of her & brought her off from the Shore. She proved to be the Sloop *Mary* of Bequia in ballast. Sunk her & made sail to Northward.

Midnight pleasant. Tacking Ship occasionally in and off Shore. At 7 AM discovered a Sail in the Northern quarter. Made all sail in chase. At 11 AM boarded the Swedish Sloop *Wasp* of St. Barths bound to Grenada. Examined her & let her pass. At Meridian East end of St. Vincents bore ESE dist. 4 leagues. Lat Obn 13 29 North

Remarks on board Thursday 12th January 1815
At 6 PM the North part of St. Vincents bore SE by E distant 11 leagues & NW part of St. Lucia bore E by N 10 or 11 leagues dist. Standing to the North & Westd. At 7 PM tacked & stood to Easterly. At 7 AM the east end of Martinique[109] bore NE by E distant 10 leagues. At Meridian the harbour of Port Royal[110] bore E by N distant 12 or 13 leagues. At the same time saw the NW part of the Island. Latd Ob. 14. 19 North.

Remarks on board Friday 13th January 1815
bore SE by S dist. 10 or 11 leagues.
Midnight good Breezes & pleasant. Made several tacks in & off Shore. At 6 AM close in with the harbour of St. Pierre.[111] At 7 AM sent the Boat on Shore to procure materials for fishing the Main Mast & Main Boom. At 8 AM the Pilots Boat came on board and

returned on Shore again. Ends pleasant, laying off & on in the mouth of the Harbour.

Remarks on board Saturday 14th January 1815
At 2 PM came to Anchor in the harbour of St. Pierre with the best Bower in 30 fathoms Water and furled the sails & got all ready to fish the Main Mast & Boom. Cleared the Decks up, and 8 PM set the watch. Midnight squally. At daylight commenced fishing the Mast and sundry other Jobs of Ships Duty. Cut the first reef off the Main Sail and set the Sail Maker to work on it, got some Water from Shore. Meridian Clear & pleasant.

Remarks on board Sunday 15 January 1815
Commences with fine pleasant Weather. Carpenter and all his Crew employed in fishing the Main Mast. Boatswain Gunner & crew at sundry Jobs. Bent a new Square Fore sail.
Midnight pleasant.
Received on board 14 Casks Water 2 puncheons of Rum for Ships use. New main boom making in Shore. Ends Clear & pleasant. Making the utmost speed with our Work, several English Vessels laying off & in the harbour.

Remarks on board Monday 16 Jany 1815
Commences with pleasant Weather and fine Breeze. At 4 PM finished fishing the Main Mast & woolding it. At the same time received the New Main boom on board. All hands employed in getting ready for sea. John Ward Landsman Run away[112]
At 6 AM got underway & drifted out. Sent the Boat on Shore. At 9 AM returned, took her in & made Sail to the Southward. At 11 AM passed within half a Mile of an English Ship, but could not take possession of her and being within Neutral limits. At Meridian abreast of Fort Royal Bay.

Jan. 16, 1815 the USS *President* engaged a British squadron of four ships HMS *Endymion, Majestic, Pomone, Tenedos*. Because of the heavy squadrons and the blockade, the British could transport their troops to attack Washington, D.C.

Remarks on board Tuesday 17 January 1815
At 1/2 past Meridian passed across Fort Royal Bay. at 2 PM passed Diamond Point & Rock and saw Point Saline and the Island of St. Lucia. At 1/2 past 2 PM saw a sail near the Island of St. Lucia upon

a wind standing to the Northward. Made all necessary sail in chase. At 3 discovered her to be a Ship apparently English. She tacked Ship off our Weather bow and immediately after fired a Gun and bore up for the Land. Could plainly perceive her hoist Signals and see them answered on Shore. We tried to cut her off from taking shelter, but could not effect it. At 4 PM she being close to the Land took Shelter under a strong Battery a little to Windward of the harbour of St. Lucia. The Batteries being upon a Hill opened a Fire upon us without doing any injury. At 1/2 past 4 P.M. observed Signals answered by a Man of War Brig that was laying in the harbour of Castro.[113] She got immediately under way and gave chase to us. The Ship we supposed was a packet. At 8 PM close in with the Diamond Rock.[114] Tacked Ship and lost sight of the Man of War Brig. Midnight abreast of the East end of St. Lucia. At 10 AM discovered a small sail to windward. Gave chase.
Meridian saw the Islands of Barbadoes & St Vincents, one bearing E by S the other W by N. Were about midway between them.

Remarks on board Wednesday 18th. January 1815
Commences with light winds. Making short tacks to Windward in Chase of the small sail, a Schooner which we gained upon very fast. At 6 PM the east part of Barbadoes S by E 1/2 E, at 1/2 past 7 coming Dark & Cloudy, last sight of the chase.
Meridian Barbadoes bore WSW distant 8 or 9 Leagues lying to Windward under short sail.

Remarks on board Thursday 19 Janry. 1815
Commences with moderate Weather. Tacking alternately to N and SE under short sail, the land in sight. At 4 PM exercised the Great Guns and small Arms
Midnight as before
Latter part employed in fitting futtock Shrouds and sundry other necessary Jobs of Ship's duty. Ends clear & pleasant.

Remarks on board Friday 20th Janry. 1815
Commences with light Winds and fair weather. The Southern part of Barbadoes, bore W 1/2 N. distant 8 or 9 leagues. Tacking alternately through the night to the Northward & SE.
Midnight, winds flurry with flying clouds. At 6 AM Barbadoes W by N. Latter part employed fitting Slings & straps for the fore yard and Sunday other Jobs of Ship's duty.

Remarks on board Saturday 21st January 1815
Commences pleasant &c. At 6 PM the center of the Island bore West distant 5 leagues. Midnight heavy squalls with Rain. At 6 AM The Land in sight from the Mast head bearing W by N. Ends Moderate Breezes and pleasant weather. Employed in Sundry Jobs of Ship's duty. Latd. Obr. 13- 01 North

Remarks on board Sunday 22d January 1815
Commences with Moderate Winds & pleasant Weather. At 6 PM the Island of Barbadoes bore W 1/2 N distant 8 leagues. At 11 tacked ship, head to SE.
Midnight pleasant. At 4 AM tacked ship again head to Northward. At 11 AM made a large Sail ahead. At 1/2 past 11 tacked ship to the Northward and made Sail. Upon tacking Ship the vessel we had discovered bore up for us & made sail in chase of us.
Meridian She was discovered to be a large Ship under a crowd of Sail after us. Latd. ob. 13. 13 North.

Remarks on board Monday 23d. January 1815
Commences with fresh Trade. Ship in chase on our Weather quarter. At 6 P.M. the Ship bore S 1/2 East immediately in our wake. Dropping her fast. At 8 PM tacked head SE. At 9 lost sight of the Ship.
Midnight, flurry with fresh Breezes with considerable Swell, carrying a press of Sail. At 2 AM took in Fore top Gallant Sail and reefed Main & Main Topsail. Day light, nothing in sight
Meridian light Winds and fair Weather. Bent a New fore top Sail. Employed at Sundry Jobs of Ship's Duty. Gunner & Crew employed in making of Wads &c Lat. ob. 12. 56 North

Remarks on board Tuesday 24th Janry. 1815
Commences with Light Winds and squally with Rain. Under Short Sail. At 8 PM wore Ship head to SE
Midnight fresh breezes
Day light nothing in sight. At 8 AM wore Ship. Latter part employed in various Jobs of Ship's duty. Ends cloudy & pleasant. Lat. Obd. 12" 03 North

Remarks on board Wednesday 25th January 1815
Commences with light Winds and pleasant. At 4 PM tack'd Ship, head Southerly. At 8 PM bore up & ran down under easy sail.

Midnight moderate Breezes and pleasant. At 5 1/2 AM haul'd upon a Wind. Very squally with Rain. At 11 1/2 AM tacked ship head to the Northd. Employed in Sundry Jobs of Ship's duty. Ends pleasant Lat. ob 12- 34 North

Remarks on board Thursday 26th January 1815
Commences good Breezes and pleasant Weather. At 6 PM Barbadoes bore W by N distant 10 leagues.
Midnight wore Ship head SE. Daylight nothing in sight. At 8 AM wore Ship and bore up West. At 9 1/2 made a Sail upon our lee bow. Jibb'd Ship and gave chase. Same time made Barbadoes bearing West. At 11 AM ascertained the chase to be a (Brig) Man of War. Hauled our wind to the NW. Lat. ob 13- 01 North

Remarks on board Friday 27th January 1815
Commences Moderate Breezes and pleasant. At 4 1/2 PM carried away the Main Boom in Jibbing Ship. Set the Carpenter & crew to work to fish it. At 6 PM NW part of Barbadoes SE by S distant 5 Leagues.
Midnight finished fishing the Main Boom & got it out to its place.
Meridian Moderate Trade Winds. Clear and pleasant. North part of Barbadoes bore E by S, 5 or 6 leagues distant. Lat Obn. 13. 24

Remarks on board Saturday 28th Janry. 1815
Commences with fine Weather and Moderate Breezes. At 5 PM the South West part Barbadoes, bore NE by E distant about 11 leagues. At 6 PM tacked Ship to the Northward.
Meridian Squally with fine Rain. Latter part fresh Breezes & Cloudy. Under short sail. Ends squally with Rain No observation

Remarks on board Sunday 29th January 1815
Commences light Winds and Squally with a heavy swell from the NE. At 5:30 PM made a sail nearly ahead. At 6 tacked Ship to the Northd. At 8 lost sight of the sail. At 3 AM made a sail on our weather Beam. When we tacked Ship in Short time after we discerned she was in chase of us. We standing to the Northward with all drawing sail. At daylight found her to be nearly within Gun shot, a large Frigate which we supposed to be the *Barrossa*. From this time till 11 AM very squally with small showers of rain. Carry a press of sail, but not gaining on frigate any, she rather gaining on us.

At 1/2 past 11 AM finding the frigate still gaining on us, bore up and set every possible sail. She commenced firing on us. No obsn.

Remarks on board Monday 30 January 1815
At 1/2 past Meridian discovered land on our Lee bow. Supposed it to be Martinique. At 1 PM the North part bore South 8 leagues. The Frigate on our Weather quarter still in chase. At 2 PM the heavy & continual squalls greatly favoring the Frigate, she began to near us, in so much as to make it necessary for us to heave 10 of our carronades overboard, also some of our Spare spars off the deck & start some of our water below.[115] She still continuing firing her Guns of her Fore Castle, got our 2 long 12's aft. Sawed down the taffrail and gave the guns more Room, and commenced firing at her from our Stern Ports, apparently with some execution. At this time dropping her fast. At 3 PM made an hermaphrodite Brig on our Starboard bow. At 3.30 she passed our Bows steering SE and hoisting a Swedish Flag. At 4 PM North part Martinique bore SE 4 miles. At 7 PM lost sight of the Frigate and haul'd up SSW & after SSE. Daylight Martinique in sight. At 7 AM lost sight of the Frigate and haul'd up SSW and after SSE. Daylight, Martinique in sight. At 7 AM North West and E by N distant 10 leagues. At the same time made a sail on our Lee Bow bearing SSW. Coming up with her fast, find her to be a Brig under a press of Sail standing about West. At 11 AM the Chase hoisted Spanish colours and on our firing a Gun to leeward hove to and we soon after came up & boarded her. Lat ob 13. 07 North

Remarks on board Tuesday 31st. January 1815
Commences fair & pleasant Weather with moderate trade Winds. Lying to, overhauling the Brig, which proved to be a Spaniard from Cadiz & bound to Laguira. At 2.30 dismissed him & filled away and made sail. At 6 PM reefed Fore & Main Topsail & Main sail.
Midnight, Fresh Breezes and flawy.[116] At 10 AM the West end of St. Vincents bore E by N 6 or 7 leagues distant. Made a Sail on our Weather bow nearly ahead. Made sail in chase Lat by ob 13. 14 North

Remarks on board Wednesday 1st. February 1815
Commences with Moderate Breezes and fair Weather. In chase of the Sloop to Windward. At 1.30 tacked ship to the NE. At 3.30 the breeze increasing and we gaining on her fast, she hoisted Swedish

Colours & soon after hove to, when we came up and boarded her and found her to be of and for St. Barts. from Trinidad in ballast. At 4.20 PM discharged her. At the same discovered two sail on our Weather bow. When we sail upon a Wind in chase of the largest, a Ship steering West, the other a small sloop steering southerly. The SW end of St. Vincents SE by E and E 5 leagues. At 7 fired a Gun at the Ship when she took in her studding sails and rounded to. We hoisted a signal which she not answering gave her another Gun, upon which she hoisted a Lantern. We then steered athwart his stern, hailed & ordered him to send his Boat on board, which order he complied with. We also sent an officer on board him to overhaul. She proved to be the Ship *Sarah Maria* Captain Itter of & from Rotterdam[117] for Curacao 38 days. Cargo Sundries.

Midnight good breezes and pleasant. At 6 AM land in sight to windward bearing about East.

Meridian North part of St. Vincents bore East distant 8 leagues. Ends light winds nearly Calm. Employed in setting up the fore Rigging & other Jobs of Ship's Duty Lat. obn. 13. 17 North

Remarks on board 2d. Feb. 1815

Commences with light Winds and pleasant Weather. At 5 PM the South part of St. Vincents bore E by N distant 11 leagues. At 10 AM tacked to the Northward.

Midnight, fine breezes and clear moonlight. Working to Windward & tacking every two hours through the night .

At daylight the Granadillos Island[118] to windward. At 10 AM being in with the Granadillos made all sail in chase and soon after discovered her (chase) to be a Ship standing in a direction towards Granada. At 11 AM made Granada ahead, at the same time made another small sail on our Lee bow. Ends pleasant.

Remarks on board Friday 3d. Feb. 1815

At 1 PM could plainly discern the ship that we were in chase of was a Merchantman, apparently English. Called all hands to quarters & got all Clear for Action, and loaded the Guns with round & grape. At 2 PM drawing close to the Ship and the Land both, fired a Shot ahead and hoisted our Colours. She immediately hoisted English Colours and commenced at us, which we returned. At 2.15 she struck her colours and we ceased firing, having all her sails set studding sails &c. Hailed the Ship and requested the Captain to lay his head to the Southward, he said his men were all run below from fear. I assured him, that if they came on deck not a man of them should be hurt. He called the men on deck under the pretense of wearing and put her before the wind for the purpose of running her. We having shot considerably ahead made sail immediately and closed with him, and in about 10 Minutes layed him alongside and boarded him, his Men having all run below. Got her around to Southward and stood from the land, it being about half a Mile off. The Ship proved to be the *Corunna* of and from London bound for Grenada with Coal as Ballast and some Articles of Hardware. She was commanded by Captain Dempster, mounted 8 guns and 18 Men. Took out all the prisoners and sent Mr. John Powers Prize Master and 11 Men to take her to the United States. Midnight bore up and run West under easy sail. At 8 AM discovered a Ship on the Weather bow, apparently a Ship run away before the wind. Made sail in chase. Made a convoy; counted 110 sail, the London Convoy.[119] The Ship we supposed to be the convoy Ship, a Frigate. At 10 AM The Frigate gave chase to us. Hove about and stood for her. After a little time she hove about and stood for the Convoy. We hove about and stood for the convoy also. Meridian, supposed the Island of Grenada bore East 15 leagues. Lat. ob. 12. 20 North

Remarks on board Saturday 4th Feby 1815

Begins with fine Breezes and Smooth Sea. All sail set in chase of the Convoy. The Frigate under easy sail. At 5 PM close to Convoy and very near the sternmost Vessels. At the time the Frigate set every necessary Sail that she could and gave us chase. Tacked ship and stood from her. At 7 lost sight of her. Bore up to the Westward and then hauled to the North & westward. Midnight pleasant. At Daylight saw a ship Bearing about SSW and the Convoy about North. At 8 AM closed to her. She hoisted English colours and upon our hoisting the American Flag, she struck. Out boat and boarded her. She proved to be the Ship *Adventure* of London, Captain Crocker from London to Havanna with ballast and Iron work. She had 4 Guns and 14 Men. Took out the Prisoners and several small Articles and manned her for the United States. At Meridian we parted Company & went in chase of the convoy, which we understand is bound for Havanna, Jamaica &c.

Remarks on board Sunday 5th. Febry. 1815

At 5 PM made the Convoy bearing about N. by W. steering NNW. At Night carrying all sail necessary, at day light nothing in sight. At 8 AM made the convoy again steering more to the Northward. Several Vessels appeared to be detached from the Convoy, steering more to the Northward. Gave chase immediately. At 11 AM could plainly discern six Ships and two Brigs had separated from the Convoy for another destinations, one of the Brigs apparently a Man of War. At Meridian gaining fast on the Convoy, could discover 4 Ships apparently well armed and the two Brigs. They kept close together and made every preparation to engage us. Ends carrying all necessary sail in chase. Lat. ob 14. 53 North

Remarks on board Monday 6th. Febry. 1815
Commences fine weather and Moderate Winds. At 3 PM drawing close up on the Weather quarter of the Eight Vessels. Got all clear for Action. At 1/2 past 3 hoisted our colours and gave a Shot at the first Brig. Our shot was immediately followed by the Stern chasers of the 4 ships at us. Sheared closer to and kept firing at them and endeavoring by several maneuvers to separate them;[120] they however kept in close order firing frequently at us. We still kept dogging them drawing their fire. Discharged several of our Broad Sides at them. They sent many shot thro' the Sails & Shot away the Main top Gallant Mast. At 6 P.M made another trial (attempt) to Leeward, but finding their keeping close would in fact prevent our doing anything with them, tried again to separate them but to no purpose. Kept close to them in hopes they would separate. Bore up on them again and received several Shots but could not affect a Separation.
Midnight watch them sharp. Daylight the whole Eight in sight. Dogged them till 8 A.M. A strange sail at this time made its appearance to Leeward. Up in chase. Meridian lost sight of them. The Islands of Puerto Rico & Mona[121] in sight. Ends pleasant Breezes &c.

Remarks on board Tuesday 7th. Febry. 1815
Begins with fine Breezes and pleasant weather. At 3 P.M. Mona bore NE distant 5 leagues. Coming up with the chase which appeared to be a Pilot boat vessel apparently a Privateer. At 4 PM she hoisted Carthagena Colours.[122] We spoke her and the boat in board. She

proved to be a Privateer from Carthegena on a cruise. At 6 PM bore up before the wind, the Privateer also.
Midnight squally with rain. At Day light saw the Carthangenian astern, all sail set before the Wind. Ends squally rainy weather and heavy swell from the Eastward. Lat. by ob. 17. 17 North

Remarks on board Wednesday 8 Febry. 1815
Commences fine Breezes and pleasant Weather. Running down before the wind with all sail set. At 4 P.M. made Altwalla Rock nearly ahead; at the same time made Islands Benta and St. Domingo. At 6 P.M Altwalla bore WNW 2 leagues distant.
Middle part squally with Rain. At day light saw the convoy on our Lee beam. Took in Fore top Gallant sail, reefed. Fore top sail and hauled by the wind. At 8 saw point Abbaco[123] bearing North 8 leagues dist. At 8 jibed Ship and haul'd on a Wind to N.E.
Meridian all necessary sail set by the wind. Ends pleasant. Employed at sundry Jobs of Ship's duty.

Remarks on board Thursday 9th. Febry 1815
Commences with light Showers of rain, the convoy in sight to windward. At 3 P.M. jibed Ship. At 6 the Island of St. Domingo to the North and the Convoy in sight to westward. At 8 PM lowered the Main sail down, and set studding sails each side below and aloft. Midnight fine Breezes. At 3 A.M. shortened sail. At day light made the convoy close to us. Discerned a sail. Made all sail on chase. At AM could discover her to be a Ketch apparently English.
Meridian coming up with the chase fast. She appeared to be Armed. Ends clear and pleasant. Lost sight of the Convoy.
Lat. by obn. 16. 46 North

Remarks on board Friday 10th. Febry. 1815
At 2 P.M. coming up with the chase, she hoisted English Colours and hauled up his Foresail. We hoisted our colours & running alongside fired a Volley of Musketry into her, when she struck. She proved to be the Ketch *Martin* from Kingston, Jamaica, & bound to Aruba.[124] Took out the Prisoners and some Provisions &c and burnt her.
Middle part Moderate breezes and pleasant. At 7 A.M. made a sail on our weather beam. Made all sail in chase. At 8 A.M. made another sail 3 points afore the weather beam. Latter part fresh

breezes and Squally with smart showers of Rain. Ends in chase of the first sail, a Schooner. Lat. obn. 17. 20 North

Remarks on board Saturday 11 Febry 1815.
Begins fresh breezes and squally with heavy Sea. At 1.40 P.M. the Chase hoisted Spanish Colors and bore up for us. She was from Kingston Jama. bound to the City of St. Domingo. Put 4 Prisoners from Ketch *Martin* on board of her & made sail to the Westward in quest of two Sail. At 3 P.M. Cape Liberoon bore ENE 11 leagues. At half Past 3 made the sail to leeward again carrying all Sail in Chase. At 7 lost sight of the Chase.
Midnight squally with Rain. At Daylight fill'd away and made Sail. A Sail in sight on the N.W quarter. Made Sail in Chase & Soon after discovered her to be standing for us when we tacked. At same time saw East End of Jama. bearing N by W. At 11 AM. made a Small Sail to windward running down before the wind, apparently, a small schr. with square Sail set. Ends fresh breezes & squally with heavy sea & some rain. Lat. obsn. 17. 55 North

Remarks on board Sunday Febry. 12, 1815
Commences fresh breezes and squally. Beating to windward in sight of Jama. At 1 P.M brought to a small sail a Schr. under Spanish Colours. Out Boat and boarded her. While overhauling her made another sail to windward running down. At 2 PM discharged the Schooner. The Last Sail, a small schooner also, coming down upon us hoisting Spanish Colours & hove to. Out Boat & Boarded him. He was from Porto Rico bound to Kingston Jama. At 3 discharged him and made sail by the wind. At 4 bore up before the wind to the Westward. At 5 brought to a small Sloop under English colours from Kingston bound to Turk's Island[125] in Ballast. At 6 P.M discharged her.[126] At same time Morant Point[127] bore SW 5 leagues distance. At daylight saw a large ship bearing NE. Light winds inclining to Calm. Tacked and made sail in Chase. At 9 the Chase, a Ship, hoisted English colours aft and a signal forward. At this time Arenatta Bay bore South 3 or 4 leagues distance. Lat. obsd 13. 40 North

Remarks on board Monday Febry. 13, 1815
At half Past M. running up along side the Ship hoisted the Yankey flag, when she struck. Boarded her, & found her to be the *Mary and Susanna*, King, from London for St. Anns Jama.[128] Cargo of

sundries, dry goods & 6 guns & 22 men. Took out the prisoners, and commenced taking out the Cargo. At 6 PM Aranatta Bay bore South 11 leagues Distance. Put Mr. Coffin and a prize crew on board and ordered her to keep Company with us. Steering all night to the west. Middle part squally with rain. At daylight the Island of Cuba in sight. Light weather. At 8 AM Cape Cruz,[129] bore NNW dist. 9 leagues. Commenced taking out cargo from the Prize again and stowing it away in us. Meridian pleasant. Continuing to take out goods from the Prize.

Remarks on board Tuesday, 14th. February
Begins moderate and Cloudy. Laying to take out goods from the Prize. At 6 P.M Cape Cruze bore North 8 leagues Dist. At 7 fill'd away under Short sail in company with the Prize, standing to the Westward. Midnight squally. Daylight nothing in sight. Began to take out Cargo from the Prize, laying by for that Purpose. At Meridian saw Cap Cruz bearing NE 10 leagues dist. Ends light winds and cloudy. Latd. Obsd. 10. 29 North

Remarks on board Wednesday 15th. 1815
Begins light winds and squally. Lying by in company with the Prize.—At 6 P.M. parted Company with the prize, both of us making all necessary sail to the Westward. At 8 AM. made the land on our weather bow and hauled up for it. Found it to be the Cayman Brake (Brac)[130] & soon after saw the little Cayman Island.
At Meridian West end little Cayman bore N.E. 8 Leagues distance. Ends Moderate breezes & pleasant weather. Employ'd at Sundry jobs of Ship's duty. Lat. obsd. 19. 36 North

Remarks on board Thursday 16th. 1815
At 3 P.M made 3 Sails bearing SE. Made all sail in Chase. At 4 P.M. came up with and boarded them, 2 Ships under Hamburg colours and a Brig under Russian Colours, all bound to the Havanna from St. Thomas. At 8 P.M. discharged two of the Vessels, on board of which by permission of the Capt. put the 7 Prisoners, officers of Different Prizes. At 11 P.M. discharged the other Ships on board of which (by permission) we put 4 prisoners.
Midnight moderate breezes and cloudy. At 3 AM wore Ship, head SE. At 6 AM saw the Island of Grand Cayman bearing North distance 4 leagues. At 10 hove to close in shore on the SW side of the Island and sent 3 Boats on shore with 31 Prisoners near

Georgetown[131] and Gave them four barrels of Provisions. Meridian pleasant. End cloudy, lying to near the land.

Remarks on board Friday February 17th 1815
At 1 P.M fill'd away and stood to the Southward under easy sail. At 4 PM SW part of Grand Cayman bore S by E dist. 6 leagues.
Midnight squally with rain. Daylight nothing in Sight. Moderate wind and Cloudy. Every drawing sail set.
Meridian clear and pleasant weather, with moderate trade winds. Carrying all necessary Sail. Employ'd at sundry jobs of Ship's duty Latitude obsd 20. 48 North

Remarks on board Saturday 18th. Febry. 1815
Commences moderate winds with clear and pleasant weather, all necessary sail set. At 6 PM shorten'd sail.
At 8 A.M saw 3 sail bearing about NE.
Meridian made the land bearing WNW. Ends light airs of wind from the Eastward. Employ'd scraping and painting the vessel outside & sundry other jobs of Ship's duty. Latd. Obsd 21. 34

Remarks on board Sunday 19th. Febry. 1815
Begins light winds and sultry weather. All necessary sail set, standing in for the land. At 4 P.M saw a low point of land bearing WNW at same time could distinguish the three sail in sight to be the same which we boarded on the 16th inst bound to the Hava. At 6 P.M tack'd Ship, Cape Coruntes[132] then bearing S.E dist. 5 miles and the False Cape WNW 6 leagues. Took in foresail & fore Royal & backed the Topsail. Drifting S.W 1/2 knot pr. Hour. Daylight nothing in sight. Fill'd away, and made sail by the wind to the NW. At 6 AM saw the land bearing NW to ENE. Cape Antonia[133] bearing W by N 1/2 N. At 10 being close in with the land sent 2 boats on shore to look out for water. Ends pleasant, lying to for the Boats. Latd. obsd. 21. 50 North

Remarks on board Monday Febry. 20th. 1815
At few minutes past Meridian made a sail in the SW quarter, when we made a signal for the Boats, which signal being promptly attended to, we were soon after under a press of sail in chase. Gaining on the Chase find her to be a Schr. standing to the SE. At 2 P.M. Cape Antonio bore N. by W 1/2 W 6 or 7 leagues dist. At 2.40 the Chase in studg. sails &c. and haul'd by the wind. At 3 hoisted

Spanish King's Colours and soon after (we being nearly within musket shot) she hove to. She appeared to be a fast sailing pilot boat schooner. Boarded her and found her to be from Campeache[134] for St. Iago. de Cuba. Cargo Indigo Logwood &c. Took out 7 Seroms of Indigo, which were for English Acct. At 6.30 suffer'd her to proceed.
Midnight Moderate winds and clear weather. Made the land ahead, and tacked to the Southward. Same time backed Main Top Sail. At 4 A.M fill'd away and streach'd off to the southd. At 5 tack'd again and stood in for the land.
Meridian pleasant weather. Close in with the Cape Antonio. Sent 2 Boats on shore. Latd. Obsd 21. 50 North

Remarks on board Tuesday 21st. Febry. 1815
Commences moderate breezes and pleasant weather. Laying off and on the Cape. At 3 P.M. the Boats returned on board bringing a great quantity of excellent Crawfish, some sea Fowl &c. At 5 stood off from the Land. At 6 Cape Anto. bore N by W 1/2 W 3 leagues dist. At 10 fresh breezes. Shortened sail. Midnight pleasant, standing off and on shore alternately thro the night. Daylight nothing in sight. At 6 A.M. made the land bearing from NE to NW by W. At 7 being close in with Middle Cape jibed Ship and stood down along shore.
At Meridian Cape Antonio bore North 4 leagues distance. At Meridian Cape Antonio bore North 4 leagues distance. Ends pleasant weather. Employ'd at Sundry jobs Ship's duty.
Lattd. obsd 21. 46 North

Remarks on board Wednesday 22nd. Febry. 1815
Begins fresh breezes and clear weather. Laying off & on in Sight of Cape Antonio. At half Past 3 p.m breeze freshening on us and a considerable swell running. Housed the Guns[135] on both sides. At 4 standing to the Southward on the larboard Tack, made a Sail on our weather bow apparently before the wind Cape Anto. then bearing NW by N 4 or 5 leagues distance. At 6 took in main Top Sail and took a 2nd Reef in fore T. Sail. Gaining on the Chase make her out a small Felucca Rigged Vessel[136] standing to the Southward. At 7 lost sight of her & tacked to the Northward.
Midnight more moderate. At 1 AM. wore Ship, head SW & at 4.30 wore to the Northward. At daylight 10 or 12 sail in Sight to the Southd. Directly afterwards discovered near one hundred sail.

Middle Cape then about NNW dist. 6 or 7 miles. Bore up & run to the NW. At 8 Cape Anto. bore SSE 1 mile distance. At 9 hove to head NE. At 10 fill'd away. Ends fresh breezes lying by. Some of Convoy in light astern. Latd. obs. 22. 19 North

Remarks Thursday 23rd Feby 1815
Begins moderately and fair, under short sail standing to the Northwd. About 100 Sail in Sight to the Southwd. At 6 PM the body of the convoy bore SE by S. No land in sight. A few minutes before 8 tack'd to the NE. At 10 was the Convoy again.
Midnight as before. Daylight all the Convoy in sight standing to the NE. At 8 AM came up nearly within gun shot of the convoy and continued to maneuver in such a manner as to be Enabled to reconnoiter them. At 11 AM the commodore's Ship, a 74, gave Chase to us but finding we beat her with ease, she gave up the chase and tack'd ship for the Convoy, which bears about ENE in sight from aloft. At same time leaving a Ship under our Lee, apparently a Sloop of War. Ends pleasant. Employ'd at Sundry Jobs.
Lattd. Obsd 23. 16 North

Remarks on board Friday 24th. February 1815
Commences Moderate and fair Weather, all the convoy in sight. At 5 P.M tack'd to SW. steering that Course half an hour. At 5.30 tack'd to the N.E. At 11 P.M. Convoy in sight off the Lee quarter. Midnight as before, but no ship in Sight. Hove the main Topsail to the mast. 1 AM bore up and run down half an hour, when we again backed the main Top Sail, and at 2.30 AM. made the Convoy to the westward nearly in our wake. Kept sight of him until 3, when we fill'd away on a wind running a head of them. At 5 tack'd ship and stood to the Southward of the Convoy, which appeared close together and no stragglers. At 10 tack'd to the southward, passing close along by the whole Convoy reconnoitering them. At 11 tack'd to the NE.
Meridian all the convoy in sight on our lee beam. Employ'd at Sundry Jobs of Ship's Duty. Lattd obsd. 23. 49 North

Remarks on board Saturday 25th February 1815
Commences moderate. Standing to N.E., the Convoy close under our lee. At 3.30 P.M a Ship of War tack'd to the Southward, apparently in Chase of us. Tack'd at same time.

At 4 P.M. the Ship tacking we tack again also. At 5 squally with rain, ahead reach'd the Ship very fast. At 8 lost sight of the convoy, and made them again at 9.
Midnight as before. At 2.30 AM tack'd to the NE. Daylight the convoy in sight off our Bow. At 7 AM tack'd to the southward. At 8 A.M having a regular breeze employed trimming ship by shifting guns, men &c. heaving log at same time frequently. At 11 AM a strange sail in sight to the Southwd.
Meridian light winds and fair weather. Convoy all in sight. Made the land bearing from SSE to SSW. Lattd. obsd 23. 33 North

Remarks on board Sunday 26th. Febry. 1815
At half Past meridn. made a Sail nearly a head, between us and the land; at 2 P.M made a sail to windward apparently running down with the land; at 2.30 came up with and boarded her, a Spanish Schr. from Hava. for Matanzes[137] in Ballast. Discharged her in a few minutes & kept away in order to get sight of the convoy again. 3.30 made two sail bearing North. Jibed Ship and hauled up for them. At 4 P.M the Pen. of Matanzas bore SSE 6 leagues distance. Between 4 and 5 P.M. brought to and boarded both the above Vessels, a Spanish sloop & schooner from Hava. bound to Windward in ballast. At 6 P.M, bore up. Midnight squally, rain &c. Daylight nothing in Sight. At 8 AM made the Land. At 9 brot. to and boarded a Span. Schr. from Hava. to Matanzes in Ballast. At 10.30 made a sail to windward apparently a square Rigg'd Vessel running down with the Land, & soon after another sail farther to Windward. At 11.30 boarded the first sail. Russian Brig, from Havre de Grace (France) for Hava. in ballast. Discharged her in few minutes and made Sail in Chase of the other Sail; a schr, apparently a long Pilot Boat built vessel, running down before the wind.
Meridian. The chase in studding sails and hauled up a little. Havana bearing about South no great dist. off. Ends pleasant &c.

Remarks on board Monday 27th 1815
At 1/2 past Meridian. Schooner hauld more to the Northwd. carrying a press of sail. At this time also she carried away her Fore top mast, but very soon after cut and cleard away the wreck of it. At 1/4 before 1 P.M. fired a gun and hoisted the Am. flag to ascertain if possible the national character of the chase. He showed no colours but trimmd his sails close to the wind. At 1 P.M. drawing up to her

very fast she fired a Stern Chase Gun at us and hoisted English Colors, showing only 3 Ports in the sides next to us. Under the impression that she was a Runner[138] for the Hava. weakly arm'd & mann'd, used every effort to close with him as quick as possible. Saw but very few men on her deck. Hastily made but small preparation for Action expecting no fighting. The preparation was not complete at 1.25, being within Pistol shot of him, he opened a tier of 10 ports of a side and commenced firing his broadside. We immediately opened our Battery of great guns and began with the musketry, and endeavour to close for the purpose of Boarding. Moving quick at the time we shot ahead under her. He put his helm up for the purpose of sheering across our stern and giving us a raking fire, which was prevented by our timely noticing his intentions and put our helm up also. He gathered way, we closed within ten yards of him. At this time both fires were very severe and destructive and we found we had an heavy enemy to contend with, his men having been concealed under the Bulwarks.[139] Saw the blood run freely from the scuppers.[140] Gave the orders for boarding, which were quick & cheerfully obey'd. At 1.40 put helm to starboard and endeavored to lay her along side. In the act of boarding he surrender'd, tho' Mr. Christie got onboard him. Out boat and sent him on board, she proved to be H. B. Majesty's Schr. *St. Lawrence* commanded by Lieut. Jas. E. Gordon, formerly the famous Private arm'd Schooner *Atlas* of Phila. mounting 15 guns, fourteen 12 lb Carronades & a long nine. Allowd a complement of 75 men. Had on board a number of marines, and some Navy Gentlemen passengers bound to the Squadron off N. Orleans. By his commander's report, having 6 men killed, and 17 Wounded, many mortally, and by various other reports 15 killed, and 19 wounded. She was a perfect wreck in her hull, and had scarcely a sail or rope standing. We suffered considerably in the Sails and Rigging; had 5 men kill'd & 7 wounded, four very severely, that will be maim'd for life: their names are Thos Davis, Aquilla Weaver, Peter[141] and Yankey Sheppard.

Commenced taking out the prisoners and repairing Damages. Sent a Crew on board to assist Mr. Christie in Keeping company with us for the Night. In the course of the night her main Top Mast fell over the side, and at light the Mn. Mast went by the Board. Sent the boat on board at 9 AM to take a complete survey of her. In the course of the forenoon 3 of their wounded men died. Ends moderate. All hands Employ'd at Sundry Jobs. Took out some purser's slops from the *St. Lawrence.* Lattd. Obs 23. 57 North

Remarks Tuesday 28th Feby 1815
Begans light airs of wind and warm weather. At 1/2 past M.. finding the great trouble and inconvenience of sending the *St. Lawrence* to the U. States, as well as the danger, She being dismasted & otherwise a perfect wreck from the action, from motives of humanity to their wounded & the solicitation of her officers, I agreed to make her a Flag of Truce to carry the wounded to the Hava. to mitigate the suffering of their unfortunate situation; the Commander of her pledging his most sacred Parole of Honour, as a British Officer for himself and in behalf of his other officers, and wounded not to take up Arms against the U. States, unless regularly exchanged in the event of him recovering from their wounds. The legality of which, however, was to be left to his government to decide.
At 1 P. M commenced putting on board the wounded we had taken out, and heaving overboard her Guns. At 4 P.M had finished with them and put on board twenty other Prisoners taken from different Vessels, and sent on board some Shirts and two Bales of purser's Slops for the comfort and convenience of the wounded and others. At 6 PM the commander in company with Mr. Rapp, my officer to whom I had given charge of the flag, went on board. Tho' before leaving the *Chasseur.* Lieut. James E. Gordon late commander of the *St. Lawrence*, express'd to me his gratiude for the generous, kind and humane treatment he and his surviving officers had experienced, acknowledging, that should it ever be our unfortunate lot to be captured during the present war, our treatment would not probably be as Satisfactory as his.
At 8 P.M. both made Sail. Kept close to him all night. At 9 AM found them Rigging additional Masts on board the *St. Lawrence* to help her progress. People employed at sundry necessary jobs of Ship duty such as repairing and bending new sails and repairing the rigging Lattd obsd. 24. 42. North

Remarks on board Wednesday 1st. March 1815
Begins squally. Employed fishing Main Boom which had been wounded by a round Shot in the late action. The prize in sight in the

NW quarter. At 2 P.M lost sight of her. At 4.30 a water spout[142] pass'd very near us to leeward. At 5 a very fresh breeze from the Nd & Wd. Handed the Main and close reefed the Fore Top Sail, and sent down fore Royal. and main Top G. yds. Midnight light airs from NW and clear weather. Daylight squally with heavy showers of rain. At 6 A.M. made land to windward bearing ENE. Made sail by the wind. At 6.30 made a sail in the wake of the land. At 8 the weather clearing a little out reefs and made all Sail requisite. 8.30 tack'd to NE. From 10 to 11 A. M. Kept our Main Top-sail aback[143] for the Sail (a ship) to come down on us, which she appears to be doing. At 11 fill'd away, the main topsail and tack'd to S.E. keeping close on a wind. At this time finding the water discolored tried a cast of the lead and struck soundings in ? fathoms water. Meridian. Another sail in sight. Ends cloudy. Employ'd as requisite.
Lattd. by an uncertain Obsd 24. 34 North

Remarks on board Thursday 2 March 1815

Begins cloudy. Two sail in sight to the westward. 1 P.M two more Sail in sight to the Northwd. At 2 P.M tack'd to the SE when one of the sail, an hermaphrodite Brig hauld by the Wind, apparently in chase of us. At 2h.30m the Ship keeping in such Shoal water as to prevent our approaching her, back'd our Mn. Top Sail for her to come down to us. At 6h 30m boarded her and found her to be from Cadiz, bound to Hava: out 74 Days. 6.30 discharged the ship and fill'd away by the wind to the Nd and Ww.
Midnight pleasant weather
At 1.30 A. M. sounded in 10 fathoms water and afterward continued to sound occasionally thro' the Night.
At daylight found our selves near the Bemini Isld.[144] & haul'd off NW. At 8 made a sail ahead standing by the wind to the Southd. which we soon discovered to be our prize, the *St. Lawrence.* Came up and boarded her.
Meredn. still in company. The NW part of the Bemini Isld. bore S.E. by E dist 4 leagues. Lattd. Obsd 25. 46 North

Remarks on board Friday 3rd. March 1815

Commences with fresh breezes and fine weather. At 1 P.M Saw the great Isaacs[145] bearing ENE. At 6 PM. NE saw G. Isaacs[146] bore SE by S 2 leagues.

Midnight Moderate winds and pleasant. Lying by with the head yards aback.
Day light nothing in Sight. Meridian light winds and pleasant. Ends lying by. Employ'd as requisite. Lattd Obsd: 27. 21 North

Remarks on board Saturday 4th. March 1815
Commences Moderate winds & fine weather. Lying by drifting along the Channel.
At 3 A.M fill'd away the head yards and Back'd the Mn. Top sail.
At 6 A.M. saw a sail on our weather bow, a Brig standing to the southwd. under a press of Sail. Set all necessary Sail by the Wind in Chase. At 8 AM tack'd Ship; at 9 brought to the Brig, a Russian, from St. Petersburg via Brook Haven Ireland (where she put in distress) and bound to Amelia Island. Cargo, Iron &c.
Meridian discharged her. Ends pleasant. Employed at sundry jobs- Ends pleasant—Employed at sundry jobs. Lattd. Obsd 29. 27 North

Remarks on board Sunday 5th. March 1815
Began moderate and fine weather. At 1 P.M. fell in with a spar. Out Boat and towed it a long side when we found it to be the Mn. Boom of *St. Lawrence*—having no occasion for it, left it adrift.
Midnight as before.
Daylight nothing in Sight. All this 24 hours under Short Sail, Mn. Top Sail aback, endeavoring to forelay[147] for the Convoy which we supposed to be to the southwd. of us.
Meridian pleasant. Employed drying Studding Sails &c. Lattd. Obsd 29° 58' North

Remarks on b. Monday 6th. of March 1815
Begins pleasant weather, Lying with Mn. Top Sail aback. At 1.35 P. M. tack'd ship to S.W. making all necessary sail. At 4.30 made a Sail about 2 points on our weather bow apparently by the wind. At 5 made another Sail 3 or 4 points on the weather bow. At 6.15 lost sight of both sail & tack'd to the SE. At 7 Shortened sail squally with rain.
Midnight clear weather still under Short Sail.
Day light nothing in sight. At 9.40 A.M. Peter (Clark) died of the wounds which he received in the late action with the *St. Lawrence*.
Meridian fine. Moderate weather. Under easy Sail. Employed as Requisite. Lattd. Obsd 30. 00 North

Remarks on board Tuesday 7th. of March 1815
Begins light Winds and fair weather under easy sail. Midnight as before. Top Sail settled down on the Cap. At 2 PM took in Mn. Top Sail, and let her F Top Sail and F Top Mast Stay Sail. Daylight moderate Breezes and cloudy, took 2 Reefs in F Top sail. At 9 A.M. coming on to blow fresh with rough Sea, hous'd all the guns, and sent down F Royl & Mn. Top gall. yd', and sent down F Royl and Mn Top Gall and hous'd F Royal mast.
Meridian Still Blowing fresh. Under close Reef'd Top Sails and F. Top Mast Stay Sail. No Observation

Remarks on board Wednesday 8th. March 1815
Commences fresh breezes and Rough Sea. Under Short Sail. At 3 P.M. set Storm Trysail.
At 6 set the Lug fore Sail[148] with a reef in it.
At 10 handed the Fore Top Sail.
Midnight more moderate, with increasing Sea. At 1 A.M the Stern Boat striking being adrift, cut away the davit falls and let her go. Day light, weather as above, nothing in Sight. At 10 AM made a sail about 4 point on the weather Bow, which we soon discover'd to be a Brig, apparently standing for us. We bore up for about 20 minutes and then haul'd by the Wind again. At Meridian Brig in sight off our Weather quarters. Wore round on the other tack and made Sail in Chase. Ends fresh breezes and squally, with continued heavy swell from the NE. Lattd. Obsd. 30. 31 North

Remarks on board Thursday 9th. March 1815
Commences fresh breezes and cloudy with Rough sea. The chase in Sight on our weather Bow, we gaining on her. At 6.30 coming dark and squally lost sight of the chase. Midnight more moderate weather, smoother Sea. Made more sail. Daylight nothing in sight. Still cloudy, but Moderate weather.
Meridian light winds and hazey Weather. All sail Necessary set. People employ'd at sundry and Necessary Jobs. Lattd. Obsd 32. 5 North

Remarks on board Tuesday 10th March 1815
Commences light Winds and hazy weather. All necessary Sail set. Midnight light airs of Wind from the Northwd & Westwd. At 2 AM a good breeze springing up, tack'd Ship's head to the NE. In F. Top gallant sail and flying Jib.

Meridian light winds and pleasant weather employd as requisite. Lattd. Obsd. 33. 30 North

Remarks on board Saturday 11th March 1815
Commences light winds and hazy weather. At 6 P.M. Nearly calm. At 8 haul'd up the square foresail and lowered down the Mn. Sail.
Middle and Latter part calm, with hazy weather.
Meridian as above. Employ'd repairing Sails and Sundry other Jobs. Lattd. Obsd. 33. 35 N.

Remarks Sunday 12th. March 1815
Commences light airs from the southwd. and hazy weather. All necessary Sail Set.
Midnight Moderate breezes and cloudy. At 2 AM brisk Gales and clear weather. At 4 Took a Reef in the Main Top Sail.
Day light nothing in sight. Warm and hazy weather. Meridian light winds, and ditto weather. Lattd. Obsd. 35. 55 North

Remarks on board Monday 13th March 1815
Commences light winds, and warm hazy Weather. Water heat by Thermometer 76°.
Day light, winds light and foggy. Water apparently discolored and colder than the air by more than one Degree pr. Thermometer, from whence we judge ourselves on the Edge of Soundings.[149] At 4 A.M. the Thermometer fell to 70.° degrees in the water. At half past 4 the Thermr. in the water fell to 60°. Lattd. Obsd 37. 42 North

Remarks on board Tuesday 14th. March 1815
Commences with Moderate breezes and hazy weather. All sail set. At 2 P.M. the breeze freshening, took in fore Top Mast & Top Galt studding sail. At 2.30 Reef'd Main Top Sail. At midnight took in Sail Tried for Soundings; got no Bottom. At 1 AM handed the Mn Top Sail and sent down Mn. Top galt yard. Blow very fresh and squally. At 2 handed square fore Sail and took the 3rd reef in the Mn. Sail. At 3 handed Fore Top Sail. At 4 sent down mn. Yard & Rigg'd in Flying Jib Boom. Day light more moderate, with heavy Swell. At 10 made 2 sail to leeward and 1 to windward. Made more Sail. At 10.30 made another Sail on our lee bow; all apparently Square rigg'd Vessels. A Brig and Ship in Sight to Leeward. And an Hermaphrodite Brig on our weather quarter apparently in Chase of us. Ends light winds and rough Sea. Lattd. Obsd. 39. 0"6 North

Remarks on board Wednesday 15th March 1815
Begins light winds and Smooth sea.
At 1 PM shortened sail and hove to for the Brig to windward (a clump of Merchantmen) to come down to us. At 2 P.M. boarded the Brig, she proved to be the *Eliza Ross* 2 days out from Boston for Richmond, She informed us of a truce having been signed by the President on the 17 Ult. At 2.30 up helm and made all Sail for the Chesapeake. At 4 Saw a Sail bearing SE of us. At 6 pass'd close by a Brig on the other Tack standing to the SE.
Midnight fresh breezes shortened sail as occasion required. Daylight still blowing fresh under reef'd Sails. At 8 AM got Soundings in 65 fathoms fine gray sand. Meridian More Moderate Weather still blowing fresh & cloudy. People employed as required.
Lattd. Obsd. 38. 24 North

Remarks on board Thursday 16th. 1815
Begins Moderate breezes and cloudy. All Necessary sail set. At 4 P.M. tack'd ship to the S.W. At 6 saw a sail ahead. Nearly calm. At 8 saw a light bearing WNW. Same time sounded in 20 fathoms water. Moderate winds and clear weath sounding frequently in 18 Fathom Water. At 3 the breeze scanting,[150] Shook the reefs out of the Main Top Sail. Daylight set lower Top mast and Top galt Studding Sails. Sent the mn. Top Galt yard up and set the sail. Several small Vessels in sight in dift. quarters. Wind very light. At 11 boarded a sloop from Fredericksburg[151] for N. York. Got some newspapers from him. In 14 faths Water. Lattd. Obsd. 37. 23" North

Remarks on board Friday 17th of March 1815
Commences light winds and fair weather; several Sail in sight. At 1 P.M saw bearing about NW. At 4 scaled off the guns. At 7 made Cape Henry Light House about 2 points on the lee bow. At 9 being in 8 fathoms water bore up for the light and fired a gun as a signal for a pilot, after which we hoisted a light, and fired several Guns at intervals.
At 11 made Old Point Comfort light bearing NW. Midnight moderate breezes and clear. At 2 AM Anchored in 6 fath water, near the Wolf Trap. Day light fresh breezes and cloudy. No pilot Boat in sight. At 6 hove up the anchor and made all sail up the Bay—Latter part fresh Breezes with rain. Made and shortened Sail as requisite. Meridian light winds abreast of Point Lookout.

Custom House Baltimore
Conts. Offs April 20. 1816
We John Dieter first Lieut. of the Brig *Chasseur* & H. P. Cathell Prize Master of the same vessel, on the cruise of which the preceding journal purports to be account of the proceedings with and on board said Brig, do solemnly sincerely and truly swear that the statement under the dates of the twenty seventh and twenty eighth February 1815 recounting the transactions on board and particulars of an engagement with his Britannic Majesty's schooner *St. Lawrence* and the immediate subsequent proceedings respecting the captured vessel, her officers, crew & passengers, is a just true report of the same as all actually occurred, to our knowledge & belief. The same being in the hand writing of Capt. Thomas Boyle Commander of the sd. brig *Chasseur*, known to the said John Dieter: and that Capt. Boyle is now absent on a voyage at sea.
  John Dieter
      HP Cathell
Sworn
Jas. U. McCulloch

After note: James Kemp built the *Comet* and *Chasseur* at his yard on Fells Point and Tom Boyle sailed the *Comet* and *Chasseur* on the successful voyages described herein.

COURT MARTIAL
of Lt. James Edward Gordon and Surviving Officers and Crew of H.M.S. *St. Lawrence*

The Court Martial assembled and held onboard His Majesty's Ship *Goree* at Bermudas on the 11th of April 1815

Present

Edward Griffith, Esquire, Rear Admiral of the White and Second Officer in Command of His Majesty's Ship Vessels at Bermudas Present,

Captains

Andrew Fitzherbert, Esquire, Commodore   Charles Dilke
Edward Dix   Charles Kerr

The Prisoners were brought into Court and the evidence and audience admitted.

Read the order of The Honorable Sir Alexander Cochrane G.C.B. Vice Admiral of the Red Squadron of His Majesty's Fleet and Commander in Chief of His Majesty's Ships and Vessels employed on the North American Station etc, etc, etc dated the 20th instant directed to Edward Griffith Esquire Vice Admiral of the White, and Second Officer in Command of His Majesty's Ships and Vessels at Bermuda, to inquire into the circumstances of the capture of His Majesty's Schooner *St. Lawrence* and to try Lieutenant James Edward Gordon and the surviving officers and crew of the said Schooner upon the spot, who were actually onboard of her at the time she was captured for their conduct upon that occasion.

Then the member of the Court and Judge Advocate, in open court and before they proceeded to trial respectively to ask the Court be directed by act of Parliament made and passed on the 22nd year of the reign of His late majesty King George, the second entitled An Act for Answering and Explanation and reducing into one act of Parliament the cause relative to the Governance of His Majesty's Ships, Vessels and forces by sea.

A Letter from Lieutenant Gordon was then read as follows; viz

Onboard the American privateer armed brig *Chasseur* off Matanzas 2nd February 1815

It is with respectful sorrow and most painful regret I acquaint you that His Majesty's late Schooner *St. Lawrence* was captured on the 26th February by the American private armed brig *Chasseur*, after an action of half an Hr about ten leagues to the westward of Havannah. The circumstances which led to this unfortunate and to me truly disastrous event are as follows:

In the expectation of orders from Admiral Cockburn to proceed to Mobile with dispatches we neared the land of Matanzas on the morning of the 26th and shortly afterwards discovered two sail under the Cuba Shore, one of which from the canvas, and otherwise suspicious appearance I considered to be an Enemy Cruiser. I progressed with belief at any other time both duty and inclination would have prompted us to close and examine her, especially as I observed her in the art of boarding a brig, but in the present instance, the importance of the dispatches with which I was charged suggests the propensity of preserving our course which was accordingly continued under every sail our spars would spread. At 11 o'clock the stranger abandoned the brig and stood for the *St. Lawrence*, and it was not long before we observed her superiority in sailing was sufficiently decided to enable her to bring us to an engagement if she thought proper. At one o'clock finding her still pursued in the chase and unable to answer the private signal I ordered the Guns to be cleared and shortly afterwards seeing that an action was inevitable I gave directions for the sails to be reduced and the schooner brought to the wind in order to preserve the weather gage. In the performance of this duty we had the misfortune to loose our fore top mast an accident in our present circumstance exceedingly unfavorable as it rendered the main top sail useless, and reduced the vessel to course which gave the enemy vessel to the courses which gave the enemy an most decided advantage in working and also enabled him to maintain a position sufficient near to command our entire deck with his musketry. The stay of the topmast being separated from forward and the schooner to balance with the top missing sails, steered large, when the enemy arrived within pistol shot of our lee quarter when our helm was put quickly to starboard and a raking fire opened from our inboard guns the enemy apparently passing to lay on board which was countered by the *St. Lawrence* recovering to man position to windward muster losing now took place and a close and destructive fire was opened from both sides a distance of forty yards and continued about 8 minutes when the brig in consequence of her weight shot ahead On pressing this interest the helm to be suddenly weatherly wore the schooner within a few yards of his stern raking him with our starboard guns and afterwards engaging him only to the leeward. The fire from our carronades was at this time quick and heavy the enemy verily took to his great guns but discharged a powerful fire from his musketry. He therefore had been successful protecting his attempt to lay us onboard which was manifestly his intention from the commencement of the engagement but I had now the mortification to find that our head sails were down and the vessel no longer governable. I also found that my officers and men aboard to the aims of about 80 muskets were falling fast, although fighting the guns on their knees. The enemy grape musketry nay even his buck shot passing every where through our covering planks which was nothing more than 3 feet in height, and 3/4 inch per board. Our fire was however continuous as our guns bore while we mustered remaining strength to show them in the ports, and for some time after they would not be run out until the enemy laid us along side, and further resistance appeared an unjustifiable waste of lives.

In this situation with every sail down, every rope cut, and the vessel lying a shattered unmanageable wreck, six of my best hands dead, myself, every officer and fifteen more wounded, without a remaining shadow of hope, or any apparent possibility of longer resistance being of further avail, I was reduced to the painful necessity of sinking my disabilities and ordering my colors to be struck-an order which occasions regret as often as it was not given while human exertion on the part of the survivors would have contributed in any further desire either to have extricated the men and vessel. When carried onboard the enemy I found her to be the *Chasseur* of Baltimore commanded by Captain Boyle whose endeavors to protect me and my officers effects from plunder and otherwise making us comfortable was such as merit our gratitude. The *Chasseur* is pierced for 22, but mounted only 14 guns, long twelve's and short nines with a complement according to the account of the officers of 153 men but by information from other sources 170 out of which she had manned three prizes the crew of which I am told amounts to 35 men. She is said to be the finest vessel with two masts out of the United States, registering up wards of 400 tons English measurement is 116 feet on Deck, and much superior to any our 18 gun brigs. Their report of their loss, as also of their numbers are excessive and contradictory. They however acknowledge 6 killed & 8 wounded. The prisoners onboard say 9 were killed and 15 wounded. Her rigging and sails are extremely shattered, but her hull is not markedly injured as we fired chiefly grape shot.

The *St. Lawrence* entered the action with 52 persons onboard including her officers, 6 passengers and as many boys, the whole of which were twelve short of her established complement. Of these five were killed, one drowned, and eighteen wounded two of which are since dead, and another not likely to live. The other are chiefly some wounds but I hope every thing from the good judgment and patience attention of Mr. Kay the Surgeon. Among the killed was Mr. Charles Cale the Gunner of H.M.S. *Callehe*, who behaved during the action with great spirit and was particularly useful. I regret these circumstances the more as I believe he has left a wife and family.

I should not be doing justice to the exertions of the remainder if I omit in this place to say they were such as offered a better choice and I ever spoke in particular of the action and able support I received from Mr. Tharp the Master who received a severe wound continued on deck to the close of the action. I would also state that the conduct of Mr. Mather who was likewise severely wounded was truly noteworthy, and such as notable as my fullest approbation.

This morning the schooners main mast has fallen by the boards which I imagine which induced the Cruizer to destroy her, and seemed impossible that she could reach an American port in safety, in her present state.

Herewith, I have added a list of the killed and wounded men. I have the honor to be
    Sir
    Your most obedient and humble servant.
    J. E. Gordon
    Late commd
    Sch. *St. Lawrence*

Killed

Mr. Charles Coles	Gunner of H.M.S. *Callehe*
Andrew Ironsides	Capt. of the hold ?
Charles Crooker	Cook
C. Ball	21st Reg.
John Learlen	Soldier of 21st Regiment
John Betten	Seaman ?

Wounded

Lt. J.E. Gordon	Severely
Mr. J. Tharp	Master severely
Mr. G Walter	Mid. severely
Mr. G. Fisher	Pilot slightly
Thomas Aveline	boy mortally -----
John Cousins	seaman dangerously
William Cook	" "
Thomas Raas	" severely
John Haususon	" "
Philip Handee	" "
John Pearson ------	"
Hugh Brown	Soldier 21 regt "
Martin Christian	seaman slightly
William Kelly	seaman slightly
Chat. Blackware	seaman slightly
Jos. Mabo	seaman slightly
Richd Swanson	seaman slightly
Thos. Greeg.	seaman mortally wounded

John Kay act. Surgeon ?
J.E. Gordon St. Lawrence (Lt. & Commd)

The President then asked Lt. Gordon whether he had anything to state against either officers or men under his command for their Conduct as it related to the defense of the *St. Lawrence* to which he replied "the whole of them did their duty," and the officers and crew being addressed by the President to the same effect stated that Lt. Gordon did all he could to defend the vessel.

Lieutenant Gordon remained in court

All the witnesses withdrew but Mr. James Tharp, the Master, who being sworn was asked the following question by the court.

You have heard Lieutenant Gordon's statement of the action read; is that to the best of your knowledge and belief a true and correct account?

Ansr- It is but I think the length of the engagement was something more than half an hour.

Were you taken onboard the Enemy vessel after capture?

Ansr- I was

Had you an opportunity of ascertaining the force of the Enemy's vessel? if so state what it was.

Ansr- Fourteen guns-viz four long 12 pdrs, four short twelve's- and the other six were 9 lb. carronades. Her crew I heard from the Prisoners were composed of 110 men and they appeared to have at best that number.

Was every thing done in your opinion by Lieut. Gordon to defend the *St. Lawrence* and to maintain the honor of the British flag?

Ansr- Every thing that possibly could be done.

After the action commenced, and you found the Enemy so superior to you could the *St. Lawrence* have got away from the Privateer?

Ansr- No, we had carried away the foretop mast steering our course, when the Enemy was within grape shot.

Has the Enemy very much the superiority of you in point of sailing?

Ansr- She had.

Since you and the remaining part of the crew have been prisoners have they all conducted themselves obediently respectfully to you and their commander?

Ansr- Yes they have.

What did the crew of the *St. Lawrence* consist of?

Ansr- forty eight at deck quarters, including officers, boys and passengers.

Do you know that the dispatches with which Lieut. Gordon was charged were actually thrown overboard?

Ansr- Rees the 2d pr. at the helm had charge of the dispatches, and I believe threw them overboard.

How often used the crew of the *St. Lawrence* to be exercised at quarters.

Ansr- At least once a fortnight depending on the weather. We frequently fired at a mark.

Neither the Court nor Lieut. Gordon desires to interrogate Mr. Tharp further, he withdrew; also Mr. John Walter, Midshipman was called in and sworn.

The Court then sent the following question to him.

You have heard Lieut. Gordon's account of the action as read; is it the best of your knowledge and belief a correct and true statement?

Ansr- It is.

Were you taken onboard the Enemy after capture?

Ansr- I was.

Have you an opportunity of ascertaining the Enemies forces? If so state what it was.

Ansr- I heard the people say she had 120 men on board at the commencement of the action. She had 14 guns viz four long 12 pounders four twelve lb. carronades- and six 9 lb. carronades.-

Was every thing done in your opinion by Lieut. Gordon to defend the *St. Lawrence*, and to maintain the honour of the British flag?

Ansr- In my opinion it was.

After the action commenced, could the *St. Lawrence*, on finding the enemy's great superiority have got away from her?

Ansr- No our rigging and sails were cut all to pieces and our fore top mast gone.

Had the enemy very much the superiority of you in point of Sailing?

Ansr- Yes, she had.

Since you and the remainder of the crew of the *St. Lawrence* have been Prisoners have they conducted themselves obediently and respectful to their officers?

Ansr- Yes, they have.

What did the crew of the *St. Lawrence* consist of?

Ansr- She had fifty one men at the commencement of the action. 48 at quarters on Deck, one sick, and two at the Magazine.

State the number and description of the Guns the *St. Lawrence* had onboard.

Ansr- Fourteen 12 lb. carronades & one long nine.

Do you know that the dispatches with which Lieutenant Gordon was charged were actually sunk?
Ansr- I do not I was at the foremost Guns.
How was the nine pounder mounted?
Ansr- A carriage mounted chase gun.
How often used the crew of the *St. Lawrence* to be exercised at Quarters?
Ansr- Twice or thrice a week in general, and at times every Evening.
Were they ever exercised in firing at a Mark, and also with blank cartridges?
Ansr- Yes they were.
Do you consider the people expert at the uses of their big guns?
Ansr- Yes I did in exercising them.

The court did not desire to interrogate Mr. Walter further, but Lieutenant Gordon asked the two following questions.
Was the long 9 pounder of any service during the action?
Ansr- No.
Why was it not?
Ansr- She had not men to fight it.

Thomas Rees, Q Master of the *St. Lawrence* was then called into Court and sworn. The Court asked:
Was every thing done, in your opinion by Lieut. Gordon, to defend the *St. Lawrence*?
Ansr- Yes.
Were the dispatches Lieut. had onboard placed under your charge during the action?
Ansr- Yes.
Do you know how they were disposed of before the *St. Lawrence* surrendered?
Ansr- Yes, I threw them overboard saw them sink.
How often used the crew of the *St. Lawrence* to have a general exercise at Quarters?
Ansr- Once or twice a week a general exercise, and at Quarters every night.

During the short time Lieut. Gordon commanded her, did the crew fire at a mark, and with blank cartridge for their better exercise?

Ansr- Yes they fired at a mark a good many times, and often with powder only.

The President here informed Lieut. Gordon that the Court had examined every person they desired, in order to ascertain to what circumstance the capture of the *St. Lawrence* was to be attributed, and wished to know whether he proposed to call upon any one. Lieutenant Gordon replied, "as the particulars of the action which unfortunately terminated in the capture of the *St. Lawrence* is detailed at length in my official letter to the Commander in Chief. I do not concieve that a labored reiteration of the same particulars either necessary, or calculated to furnish additional information. I therefore submit the substances of that letter to the consideration of the court and humbly hope it will be manifest that every thing was done to save his Majestys vessel and to support the honour of his Colors. She was defended to the astonishment of the Enemy and I hope it will be found to the satisfaction of this Court and of my Country"

The court was then cleared and proceeded to deliberate upon it for the sentence.

The Court having mutually and deliberately weighed and considered the whole of the circumstances attending the Capture of the *St. Lawrence* was of opinion that it was occasioned by the superiority of the Enemy's forces, added to the disabled state of the *St. Lawrence* at a very early period of the action from the fall of her fore top mast, that she was defended with great skill and bravery, and was not surrendered until all further resistance must have been fruitless; it did therefore honorably acquit Lieutenant James Edward Gordon, and the surviving officers and crew of the *St. Lawrence*.

The Court was then ordered and acquitted, and sentence passed accordingly

Chas. Martys: Officiating Judge

29 Hill Street Berkley Sqr
May 15, 1815

Sir: I beg leave to acquaint you for the information of my Lords Commissioners of the Admiralty that I am (scheduled) ? as passage in HMS *Tonnant* from N. America where I had the misfortune to be captured in the command of H.M. late Schr. *St. Lawrence* on the 26th Feb—the particular of which I stated officially to Lieut. Cochrane the Commander in Chief. I beg further to state that I was tried by a Court martial assembled on board H.M. Ship *Goree* at Bermuda on the 21st of Apl for the said capture.

 I have the honor to be
Sir
your most Obdnt & Hbl Servt
J. E. Gordon (Lieut.)

After Action Letters, Accounts and Reports

Niles' Weekly Register, No. 4 of Vol. VII
Baltimore, Saturday, March 25, 1815
The *Chasseur*, Captain Boyle

This famous privateer whose "blockade" of all the "outlets, inlets, bays, rivers," &c of the "united kingdom of Great Britain and Ireland," a little while ago cannot be forgotten, returned to Baltimore on Saturday evening last from a successful cruize in the West Indies, where she spread terror, with a full cargo of valuable goods. Other particulars than those which follow will inserted in our prize lists—and we also add, by way of memorandum, a variety of extracts from the West India papers to show the daring of Boyle and the chagrin of the British! His battle with the *St. Lawrence* is an affair honorable to himself & his country—the naval renown of which, indeed, we are happy to add, has been as well supported by our private as our public armed vessels. The *Chasseur* brought in 23 prisoners.

* * *

Capture of his Britannic majesty's schooner *St. Lawrence*, lieut. James E. Gordon, commander, by the private armed brig *Chasseur*, of Baltimore, Thomas Boyle, Esq. commander.
Letter from Capt. Boyle to Mr. George P. Stephenson, one of the owners of the *Chasseur,* dated

AT SEA, March 2, 1815.

Dear sir—I have the honor to inform you, that on the 26th Feb. being about six leagues to windward of Havanna and 2 leagues from the land—At 11 A.M. discovered a schooner, bearing N.E. of us, apparently running before the wind; made every possible sail in chase, the convoy in sight from the mast head, to leeward, laying too off Havanna; at meridian, gaining fast on the chase, that appeared to be a large long, low pilot built schooner, with yellow sides—she hauled up more to the northward, and apparently was endeavoring to escape us. At half past meridian, I fired a gun and hoisted the American flag, to ascertain, if possible, the nation which she belonged to; but she shewed no colors—she was carrying a press of sail, and in a few minutes carried away her fore-topmast.

She was at this time about three miles from us—they cut away the wreck of the topmast immediately and trimmed her sails sharp by the wind. At 1 P.M. drawing up with him very fast, she fired a stern chase gun at us, and hoisted English colors, showing at the same time only three ports in the side next to us.

Under the impression that she was a running vessel bound to Havanna and weakly armed and manned, I tried every effort to close with him as quick as possible. Saw very few men on his deck, and hastily made small preparation for action, though my officers, myself and men, did not expect any fighting, of course we were within pistol shot of him when he opened a tier of ten ports on a side, and gave his broad side of round, grape and musket balls. I then opened the *Chasseur's* fire from the great guns and musketry, and endeavored to close with him for the purpose of boarding; we having quick way at the time, shot ahead of him under his lee, he put his helm up, for the purpose of wearing across our stern and to give us a raking fire, which I prevented by timely taking notice of his intention, and putting our helm hard up also. He shot quick ahead, and I closed within ten yards of him; at this time both fires were heavy, severe and destructive. I now found his men had been concealed under his bulwark, and that I had an heavy enemy to contend with, and at 1.40 gave the order for boarding, which my brave officers and men cheerfully obeyed with unexampled quickness, instantly put the helm to starboard to lay him onboard, and in the act of boarding her, she surrendered.—Mr. W.N. Christie, prizemaster, from his courage and activity got on board of her, she proved to be his Britannic majesty's schooner *St. Lawrence*, commanded by lieut. James E. Gordon, formerly the famous privateer *Atlas* of Philadelphia, built in the Chesapeake, mounting 15 guns, 14 twelve pound carronades, upon an improved construction, and a long nine; allowed a complement of seventy men, and had on board a number of soldiers, marines and some gentlemen of the Navy passengers; bound express to the squadron off New Orleans; having by the report of her commander, six men killed, and seventeen wounded: but by various other reports, 15 killed and 23 wounded, most of them badly, and several mortally. She was a perfect wreck, cut to pieces in the hull, and scarcely a rope left standing, and, by report of her commander, not an officer on board, but was either killed or wounded himself among the latter.

The C's (*Chasseur's*) sails and rigging suffered much, and from the zeal and anxiety of her brave crew to do their duty, and thereby exposing themselves, I had five men killed and eight wounded, myself amongst the latter, though very slightly. Thus ended the action in fifteen minutes after its commencement, and about eight minutes close quarters, with a force in every respect equal to our own.

The *Chasseur* mounts six 12 pounders, and eight short 9 pound carronades, (the latter taken from one of her prizes) ten of our twelve pound carronades having been thrown overboard while hard chased by the *Barrosa* frigate; and she had on board 89 men, besides several boys.

From the number of hammocks, full of beds, clothes, &c. found on board of the *St. Lawrence*, it would lead to a belief that many more were killed than were reported. The *St. Lawrence* fired double the weight of shot that we did; from her twelves, at close quarters, she fired a stand of grape,[152] and two bags containing two hundred and twenty musket balls each—when, from the *Chasseur*'s nines, she fired six and four pound round shot, having no other except some few grape. Was I to close this letter without mentioning the determined bravery of my first lieutenant. Mr. John Dieter, I should be acting very unjustly to my own feelings; my other lieutenants, Mr. Moran, and Mr. Hammond, N Stansbury as well as every other officers behaved with a firmness seldom, if ever; equaled, and, I believe, never surpassed.

Yours with respect,
THOMAS BOYLE
Mr. G.P. Stevenson, Baltimore

P.S. On the night of the 26th the maintop mast of the *St. Lawrence* went by the board; such was her wretched condition and from motives of husbandry and the solicitation of her commander, I made a flag or cartel of her to carry the wounded to the Havanna, for their better comfort and convenience as I know you would wish that I should mitigate the suffering of the unfortunate wounded. I hope you will not be displeased at what I have done—there was no other alternative but to make a cartel of her or destroy her. I should not willingly, perhaps have sought a contest with a king's vessel, knowing it was not our object; but my expectations were at first a valuable vessel and a valuable cargo also—when I found myself deceived, the honor of the flag entrusted to my charge was not to be disgraced by flight. I sent to the wounded a parcel of shirts, and two bales of purser's slops to be distributed amongst them and the other prisoners. A copy of the correspondence between the captain of the *St. Lawrence* and myself you have here enclosed as well and my letter to your friends in Havanna.

* * *

Return of killed and wounded on board the private armed brig *Chasseur*, of Baltimore, Thomas Boyle, Esq. commander, in her action with H.B.M. schooner *St. Lawrence*, lieutenant James E. Gordon, commander, on the 26th February, 1815.

KILLED—Jacob Burk, carpenter, Alexander P. White, carpenter's mate; Hugh Crea, 2d gunner; Samuel M'Connel, John Carpenter.

WOUNDED—Thomas Boyle, commander, slightly Thomas Davis, seaman, severely; Aquilla Weaver, marine, do; Thos Lauter, seaman, do; Yankee Sheppard, boy, do; Hamilton Holston, ship-steward, slightly; Alfred Vincent, do; Peter, (black man identified in other documents as Peter Clark) since dead.

TOTAL—killed and wounded 13

On Board the U.S. private armed brig *Chasseur*, February 27, 1815

* * *

Copy of a Certificate to Captain Thomas Boyle, from the Commander of His Britannic Majesty's schooner *St. Lawrence*; Dated At Sea, February 27th, 1815, On Board the United States Private-Armed-Brig *Chasseur*.

In the event of Captain Boyle's becoming a prisoner of war to any British cruiser, I consider it a tribute justly due to his humane and generous treatment of myself, the surviving officers and crew of His Majesty's late schooner *St. Lawrence*, to state that his obliging attention and watchful solicitude to preserve our effects, and render us comfortable, during the short time we were in his possession, were such as justly entitle him to the indulgence and respect of every British subject.

I also certify that his endeavors to render us comfortable, and to secure our property, were carefully seconded by all his officers, who did their utmost to that effect.

J. C. Gordon   Lieut. and Com. of His Majesty's late
                      Schooner *St. Lawrence*

* * *

Niles' Weekly Register, No. 7 of Vol. VIII
Baltimore, Saturday April 15, 1815
AMERICAN PRIZES

"His majesty's" schooner *St. Lawrence*, lieutenant Gorden, fourteen 12 lb. carronades, and one long gun, 75 men, besides a number soldiers and passengers, captured by the *Chasseur* of Baltimore, captain Boyle, after a very severe action of fifteen minutes, with a loss of about 40 men killed and wounded, the *Chasseur* 5 killed and 8 wounded, and at the request of the late commander sent into Havana for the relief of the wounded.

Ship *Adventure*, for Havana, with a valuable assorted cargo of dry goods and plantation utensils, Captured by the *Chasseur* of Baltimore, and ordered for Charleston, but unfortunately recaptured off the port by the *Severn* frigate. We called her a good prize, because her most valuable effects were taken out by the *Chasseur*.

The *Chasseur*, "the pride of Baltimore," arrived at Baltimore on Saturday evening last, and saluted fort M'Henry. She is, perhaps the most beautiful vessel that ever floated on the ocean, those who have not seen our schooners have but little idea of her appearance. As you look at her, you may easily figure to yourself the idea that air, seeming to sit so lightly upon it! She has carried terror and alarm through the W. Indies, as appears by numerous extracts from West Indies papers received by her; and was frequently chased by British vessels sent out on purpose to catch her. She was once pretty hard run by the *Barossa* frigate—but some times, out of mere wantonness, affected to chase enemy's men of war of far superior force! Among the "good jokes" that appear in these papers, is one making out Boyle to be an "Irishman!" The account of her battle with the *St. Lawrence*...is as gallant an affair as has yet occurred at sea. The *Chasseur* is full of dry goods, &c. She was proceeding to New York, when she heard the certainty of the peace and bore away for the Chesapeake—She full of costly goods.

* * *

Private Armed Vessels out of Baltimore and their Prizes, 1812 to 1815

Compiled by John Philips Cranwell & William Bowers Crane, 1940
(coauthors of *Men of Marque*)

COMET
Privateer schr.
187 tons
dimensons (length, beam, depth amidship): 90.6, 23.3, 10
Built: Baltimore 1810
110 men
2 long 9s & 10—12 pound caronades
Captain: Thos. Boyle
Lieutenant: Clement Cathell
Commissioned 7/10/12
Prizes:
    (Boyle) 35
    Adelphi, ship, retaken
    Alexis, brig, retaken
    Bowes, brig,retaken
    Dominica Packet, brig, retaken
    Endeavor, sloop, destroyed
    Enterprise, brig, ransomed
    Enterprise, schr, sunk
    Experiment, sloop, destroyed
    General Spooner, sloop, retaken
    General Wale, sloop, retaken
    Hannah, brig, ransomed
    Henry, ship, Baltimore
    Hopewell, ship, Baltimore
    Industry, ship, sent in (US)
    Industry, ship, Wilmington
    Industry, sloop, burnt
    Jackman, schr. cartel
    Jane, schr. retaken
    John, ship, Baltimore
    Little Cherub, sloop, given up
    Mary, sloop, foundered

Messenger, schr. Wilmington
St. John, schr, ransomed
Venus, schr, sent in
Vigilant, schr tender
Wilmington, vessel, Puerto Rico
9 vessels, burnt

CHASSEUR
Letter of Marque Schooner
356 tons
dimensions (length, beam, depth amidships): 115.6, 26.8, 12.9
Built: Baltimore 1810
52 men
148 men
150 men
16 long 12s
Captain: Thos. Boyle
Lieutenant: John Dieter
Commissioned 6/19/14 (New York)
Prizes:
    (Wade)—11
    Ann Maria, schr, burnt (Lic)
    Britannia, brig, Beaufort
    Galatea, ship, New Bern
    Harriet Elizabeth, schr, sent in
    Joanna, polacre, burnt
    Lark, schr, retaken
    London Packet, ship Hyannis
    Martha, sloop, cartel
    Melponeene, brig, Newport
    Miranda, schr, burnt
    William, schr, burnt (Lic)
    (Boyle)—25
    Adventure, ship, retaken
    Alert, brig, burnt
    Amicus, brig, sent in
    Antelope, brig, retaken
    Atlantic, brig, retaken
    Carlbury, ship, retaken
    Christiana, sloop cartel

Commerce, brig, Charleston
Corruna, ship, Wilmington
Eclipse, brig, New York
Eclipse, sloop, burnt
Elizabeth, schr burnt
Favourite, sloop, burnt
Fox, schr, sent in
Harmony, brig cartel
James, ship sent in
Marquis of Cornwallis, brig, cartel
Martin, ketch, burnt
Mary, schr, sunk
Mary & Susan, ship, Savannah
Prudence, brig, burnt
Reindeer, brig sent in
Speculator, brig, cartel
St. Lawrence, schr, HBM, sent in (US)
Theodore, ship retaken

Notes

[1] Announcement reprinted in the *Aurora General Advertiser*, Tuesday June 8, 1813. This newspaper was published from 1794 to 1812 at Philadelphia.

[2] The document when so wrapped would immediately sink. Both English and American war ships used this technique.

[3] Source: National Archives Microfilm Publications Microcopy 588, "War of 1812 Papers" of the Department of State. Being able to identify friend or foe at sea was a critical concern to American privateer captains and there are many tragic instances where this ability was not possible.

[4] The specific text is as follows: "When it was late at night they went out togeather into the street. The night was warm and light. To the left of the house on the Pokrovka a fire glowed—the first of those that were beginning in Moscow. To the right and high up in the sky was the sickle of the waning moon and opposite to it hung that bright comet which was connected in Pierre's heart with his love."

[5] *Maryland Historical Magazine*, ed. Frank F. White, Jr. (Vol. 53, No. 4, December 1958), 295-315.

[6] Mentioned in James Fenimore Cooper's account entitled "Ned Myers: a life before the mast," published in 1843. This is Cooper's firsthand account as a youth of his first voyage during the War of 1812. Other vessels he mentions that are part of the Log of the *St. Lawrence* are related here as well as descriptions of impressment that he witnessed in his early career as a sailor. His mastery of sailing and shipboard description are included as appropriate.

[7] Largest and most populous of the Virgin Is., in West Indies; Danish possession 1753-1917; main ports Christiansted and Frederiksted.

[8] Group of volcanic islands in Atlantic between 14°47' and 17°13'N.

[9] Territory of S.America bounded on North by Atlantic Ocean, on E French Guiana, on S Brazil and on W by Guyana an English possession 1804-1816.

[10] This is a vessel carrying the same name.

[11] This is Setubal or St. Yves, a seaport in SW Portugal.

[12] Seaport in NW Massachusetts on Cape Ann; correct spelling Gloucester.

[13] A receipt listing goods shipped that is signed by the agent of the owner; inspecting these would tell what was onboard the ship and who it was consigned to and its origin enabling privateers to make legal seizure.

[14] "Ditto" means, the aforesaid, the above, the same as before; and is indicated by a pair of small marks, used to avoid repeating a word or phrase.

[15] A petty officer of a privateer designated by the captain to take a captured vessel to a neutral or U.S. port.

[16] Seaport city on Bay of Cadiz NW of Gibraltar.

[17] Seaport city W Portugal on Taugus River estuary.

[18] A commodity in trade from West Indies consisting of wood of an angiospermous tree as distinguished from that of a coniferous tree; used in ship construction.

[19] This is a reference to damage of a part of the ship.

[20] Major fort located southeast of Baltimore at mouth of Northwest Branch of Patapsco River; site of British military actions to capture shipyards producing privateers especially Fells Point. All vessels arriving or departing Baltimore pass by.

[21] Seaport of South Carolina on Port Royal Island.

[22] Located at mouth of Cheaspeake Bay across from Cape Charles.

[23] Island in West Indies in Leeward Is.

[24] Major port of Nova Scotia on North Atlantic founded as British stronghold in 1749.

[25] Seaport on NW coast of Cuba: aka La Habana

[26] Port of E Brazil now called Recife.

[27] Seaport of North West Portugal on Douro River.

[28] Seaport of S Uruguay on N shore of La Plata estuary.

[29] Island of Azores; aka Sao Miguel.

[30] The implication here is that Boyle reserved the right to detain and capture vessels irrespective of who might be convoying them.

[31] This is a means to slow or stop the forward advance of the ship by filling sail to counter the aerodynamics of the sail; the wind would blow directly against the sail exerting a force against the forward movement of the ship.

[32] Seaport on one of the largest harbours in world on SW shore of Guanabara Bay aka Rio de Janeiro Bay 16 ½ m. long by 11 m. wide.

[33] A port SW of Halifax, Nova Scotia and base of operations for British privateers during the American Revolution and War of 1812; also, a seaport on the Mersey River estuary second to London in commercial importance.

[34] Important seaport of North England on Humber River with great exports and fisheries.

[35] Seaport city of Bahia E Brazil on All Saints Bay SSW of Recife aka Sao Salvador or Bahia.
[36] Descriptive term for the size of a vessel in terms of cannon aboard.
[37] North Sea fishing port of Scotland.
[38] Seaport city of Porto dist, NW Portugal.
[39] One of the Virgin Is. in the West Indies E of St. Thomas.
[40] Seaport SW Scotland, on S shore of Firth of Clyde.
[41] Region in N Guyana and name of river that flows into Atlantic at Georgetown.
[42] These commodities are found in many of the log entries indicative of the trade pattern, the island slave labor force worked to produce these expensive items that would be exchanged for inexpensive foodstuffs, mainly grains from the U.S. and Europe, providing the planter economy with significant earnings. Other trade commodities include cocoa and mahogany logs.
[43] Westernmost island of Lesser Antilles islands in US Virgin Islands 40 m E of Puerto Rico separated from Culebra I. on W by Virgin Passage.
[44] Pillsbury Sd. Leeward and Windward Passages.
[45] Windward Passage.
[46] The Narrows
[47] Country SW Africa with major city Luanda with chief rivers Congo and Kasai; settled by Portuguese 1575.
[48] Brazilian Island in Atlantic Ocean 250 m NE of Cape Sao Roque; discovered 1501, used as a penal colony.
[49] Town E Rhode Island on Narragansett Bay; shipbuilding and whale fishery center; bombarded, burned and pillaged by British 1775 & 1778.
[50] British colony in South of Spain at closest point to Africa; major naval installation through history.
[51] What frigate this was is not clear; possibly the *Essex*.
[52] Island in Leeward Is. aka St.-Barthelemy.
[53] Cluttered with lumber or heaped togeather.
[54] Island, Leeward Is., West Indies. Basse-Terre; founded 1627, settled in 1625 by British; aka Saint Christopher, north of Dominica; 35 m. long. Seaport on SW coast of Basse-Terre I. founded 1643.
[55] Location 18°17'N. 63°15'W. This feature is covered with brushwood and grass and lies off SW extremity of Anguilla.
[56] An island in Anegada Passage, with steep sides and jagged peaks with abundant bird life.

[57] Port SE North Carolina at confluence of Neuse and Trent Rivers W of Pamlico Sound.

[58] This is the newspaper entitled *Baltimore Patriot and Evening Advertiser*, published in 1813.

[59] Commercial city and seaport S Spain on Mediterranean sea, NE of Gibraltar.

[60] Island of Leeward Islands; aka Sombrero.

[61] Largest of Canary Is. in Atlantic Ocean 40 m WNW of Grand Canary I.

[62] Island NE West Indies in Leeward Is.; extinct volcano with sheer cliffs.

[63] A French possession of 2 large islands, Basse-Terre and Grande-Terre; Leeward Islands; 16°15'N, 61°30'W.

[64] Sail Rock, a Caribbean islet, halfway between Culebra Is. (W) and St. Thomas Island. (E) in Virgin Passage; 18°17', 65°06' W.

[65] During the European wars of the 18th century, the neutrality of Denmark gave a great impetus to the trade of St. Thomas. It was during this period that the distributing trade of the island grew up. It was held by the British in 1801 and again from 1807 to 1815, during which it was the great rendezvous site of British merchant vessels waiting convoy and protection against American privateers.

[66] Largest of British Virgin Is. West Indies 21 sq. mi. largest town is Road Town; highest point Mt. Sage 1710 ft.

[67] Port on west side of island of Nevis; near Charlestown.

[68] St. Vincent 13°15'N, 61°12'W; 87 miles west of Barbados; mountainous and wooded island with bold and rocky coasts having sandy bays providing anchorage; Kingstown is the capital on SW coast with a large harbor and renowned botanic garden (1763) from which Capt. Wm. Bligh voyaged to Tahiti to obtain breadfruit plants for the collection.

[69] St. John Island one of Virgin Islands 4 m. E of St. Thomas; 20 sq. mi.; produces bay leaves for bay rum making at nearby St. Thomas Is.

[70] Island in Atlantic NE of Florida; 15 m. long 4 m. wide.

[71] Island Windward Is., E West Indies; 425 sq. m.; capital of Martinique is Fort-de-France.

[72] Island in Windward Is. E West Indies S of Martinique & N of St. Vincent; Castries is capital of Saint Lucia.

[73] Money in coin.

[74] Yellow fever is an acute infectious disease of subtropical and tropical New World caused by mosquito resulting in jaundice and dark colored vomit from hemorrages; aka yellow jack.

[75] One of the British Virgin Is. West Indies 18°29'N, 64°24'W; with summit of Virgin Peak, 414 m high; 8 sq. m.

[76] This geographic reference is probably San Juan, there is no St. John in P.R. it could be the log keeper used English for San Juan.

[77] This place reference is possibly La Guaira a seaport town N Venezuela, near Caracas.

[78] Not shown on sources - the bay in proximity to Spanish Town is Saint Thomas Bay.

[79] A boat that plies a regular route, carrying passengers, freight and mail.

[80] Island, part of St. Christopher-Nevis-Anguilla, Leeward Islands, West Indies; 35 sq. mi.

[81] Not recovering its original shape when released after being distorted; to become warped, bent, or cracked.

[82] This possibly was the British war schooner *Pictu*.

[83] The largest island of Netherlands Antilles; chief town Willemstad; held by British 1807-15.

[84] 80 m. wide between Haiti on W and Puerto Rico on E; 6 m. long and 4 1/2 m. wide.

[85] en fluyt: a sailing vessel designed in Netherlands to transport goods with maximum of space and with crew efficiency eliminating armaments for cargo space and using block and tackle to facilitate ship handling. This specialized cargo carrier gave Dutch the lead in international trade.

[86] Spelled also Ocracoke; island off cen. N.C coast, in chain of narrow sandy islands of Outer Banks lying bet. Pamlico Sound and Atlantic Ocean; 9 sq. mi.

[87] Sir William Congreve developed an incendiary rocket that was a relatively new instrument of war in 1814 that was frightening but largely inaccurate; it consisted of an explosive charge, propellant and a launching/guidance pole; it would fire to about 9000 feet. It used black powder, an iron case and a 16-foot guide stick. Francis Scott Key, writing what would become our national anthem, coined the phrase the "rockets' red glare" after seeing them used in attack on Fort McHenry.

[88] Located on Portsmouth Island off central NC coast bet. S Pamlico Sound and Atlantic; SE of Ocracoke I.

[89] Aka Wicomico River.

[90] Also spelled pennant: any of various nautical flags tapering to a point or swallowtail and used for identification or signaling; a flag or banner longer in the fly than in the hoist.

[91] This is the Hudson River.

[92] Island at southern area of the Harbour of New York.

[93] Holding area for inbound and outbound ships where last minute details are addressed as well as inspection of vessel for anything problematical with the vessel, crew, and cargo.

[94] This was to top off the water casks prior to beginning of the voyage.

[95] One of set of fortifications on Staten Island at the mouth of New York Harbour including Water Battery, and Fort Tomkins dating from 1807.

[96] Peninsula about 12 miles south of the Narrows at mouth of New York Harbor (New Jersey).

[97] Highlands of Navesink rising to a height of 200 feet above sea level are at the landward end of Sandy Hook, NJ and were the location of early signaling since 1746. In 1828 the Federal Government constructed the first aid to navigation upon the Highlands.

[98] Seaman not mentioned in crew list of Ships Articles.

[99] Fid, a piece of wood tapered for inserting in a narrow crevice and used for tightening or securing mast elements.

[100] These consisted of the long tom and carronades.

[101] Steering sails can be positioned to guide the vessel.

[102] *Chasseur* had the following great guns on aboard for the cruise: 2 long 12 pounders -aka- Long Toms- and 10 12 pound carronades called by British "smashers." Long Toms had a long range and were used to hit the enemy from afar while carronades were used in close quarters salvos when extensive damage to rigging and upper works was needed.

Captain Boyle appears to have preferred a combination of nine- or twelve-pound carriage guns and twelve-pound carronades. A nine-pound carriage or long gun had a point blank range of 300 yards and an extreme range of 1,800 yards at six degrees elevation.

The carronade came into use in the 1790's being much lighter in weight than a carriage gun firing the same weight shot. Its advantage was its weight and the fact that it used a smaller charge of powder. It provided effective fire for boarding at short range. Aboard the *Chasseur* all guns were mounted on a single deck (weather deck) and secured and contolled by breeching ropes, train and side tackle.

Tom Boyle knew the importance of drilling gun crews and so they spent much time in drill loading and or firing at a target. Robotti and Vescovi suggest the steps of shipboard gunnery:
"Cast loose your guns"
    The lashings holding the cannons against the bulwarks (housings) were removed.
"Level your guns"

The cannon barrel was lowered so that it could be pushed through the gunport.

"Take our your tompions"

A wooden plug or canvas cover over the gun's bore to keep it dry was removed.

"Load with cartridge"

The sack of gunpowder was shoved down the end of the bore with a rammer.

"Shot your guns"

The gun was loaded with one of three kinds of shot. Round shot used to hull the enemy ship make a hole in water line or hit masts. Chain shot being two cannon balls halves attached with a chain to spin and tear through rigging and sails and grape shot being a charge of musket balls loaded into the cannon via a canister. A variant of grape shot was langradge being a loose collection of scrap iron fired to kill and maim gun crews of the enemy.

"Run out your gun"

The muzzle of the cannon was pulled through the port by train tackle.

"Aim"

Each gun captain stood right behind the gun and directed his crew to position the gun barrel properly, using handspikes and quoins. Guns were aimed by the use of primative sights placed in the barrel opening.

"Prime"

A small amount of fine gunpowder carried in a powder horn was poured into the touchhole.

"Fire"

At this order, timed with the roll of the ship, the gun captain pulled a lanyard, which triggered a flintlock that created a spark that fired the gun. In case of a misfire the flintlock was backed up by a smoldering slow match to be placed in the touch hole to fire the cartridge (powder charge). The recoil of the cannon blast was checked after firing by the breeching tackle.

[103] Port and capital of Barbados, West Indies.

[104] These are oars put through ports in the side of vessel to enable maneuvering without wind.

[105] Island in Windward Is. group, S of Saint Lucia and W of Barbadoes 18m long by 11 m wide.

[106] aka linens; a cloth made flax and noted for its strength, coolness and luster.

[107] Island of Grenadines, E West Indies, S of St. Vincent.

[108] Group of 600 small islands, Windward Is., at east end of Caribbean Sea bet. Grenada and St. Vincent.

[109] Island of Windward Is. E West Indies 425 sq mi area rising to mountainous volcano of Mt. Pelee.

[110] Town at entrance to Kingston harbour SE Jamaica.

[111] Town on Martinique, West Indies destroyed by volcanic eruption of Mt. Pelee 1902.

[112] Jerome R. Garitee comments in "The Republic's Private Navy": That landsmen were marines and that there were 10 or 15 marines aboard privateers on cruize. (Ch. 8 p. 310 note 39; the ships articles for the *Chasseur* indicates three marines by title - it is probable that others of the crew were designated to be marines when action was eminent.)

[113] Castries capital and seaport of St. Lucia Windward Is.

[114] This is Rocher du Diamant, 14°27' N, 61°03'W, a prominent islet with almost veritcal sides being 176 m high. 570 feet high south of Fort-de-France at Caribbean island of Martinique.

[115] This was a step to get rid of water carried aboard to lighten vessel using siphoning hoses.

[116] A brief gust or blast of wind; a squall; a passing storm.

[117] Large port city in southern Netherlands on both sides of Nieuwe Mass 15 miles from the North Sea.

[118] What is meant is Grenadines.

[119] This was a major movement of vessels from West Indies each year beginning from St. Thomas. During the years of Danish control its distribution trade increased and during the period of 1807 to 1815 when under English control it was the great rendezvous of British merchant vessels waiting for convoy to Europe.

[120] This is a cutting out maneuver where a ship is isolated and then attacked.

[121] Island West Indies S part of Mona Passage 80 m wide bet Haiti on W and Puerto Rice on E.

[122] Flag of the city of Carthagena on NW coast of Colombia, one of important cities of of Spanish America in 17th cent. second only to Mexico City.

[123] aka Abaco two of the Bahama Islands in Atlantic Ocean E of S Florida; Great and Little Abaco.

[124] Island off coast of NW Venezuela.

[125] This is Turks and Caicos islands; two groups of islands in SE part of the Bahama Is. and N Hispaniola.

[126] This means that the privateer *Chasseur* boarded and inspected the papers and cargo manifest for contraband and then let the vessel go.

[127] Cape at E end of Jamaica, West Indies.

[128] Town and bay on N coast of island of Jamaica, West Indies. The *Mary and Susanna* was a significant capture as judged by the time it took transfer the cargo - noon on Feb 13 to evening of Feb 15th. The transfer took place on the high seas with the vessels along side each other.

[129] E Cuba on Caribbean Sea 95 m W of Santiago, Cuba.

[130] One of island group in NW Caribbean Sea, consists of Grand Cayman, Little Cayman, and Cayman Brac.

[131] Town and capital of Cayman Is. on Grand Cayman I.

[132] aka Cabo Corrientes is a large deep water coastal indentation or bight; near western end of Cuba.

[133] aka Cabo San Antonio west end of Cuba, low and covered with trees which are visible before land.

[134] City on W coast of Yucatan peninsula.

[135] A command to secure the cannon with breeching rope to gun port at side of ship.

[136] A narrow, swift sailing vessel, propelled by lateen sails and oars.

[137] City NW part of Cuba 60 mi. E of Havana.

[138] A message runner or dispatch ship.

[139] The part of a ship's side that is above the upper or weather deck.

[140] An opening and channel in the side of a ship at deck level to allow water to run off.

[141] The ships articles and other documents suggest that the man's name was Peter Clark.

[142] This is a tornado that passes over water.

[143] Square sail positioned to catch the wind upon the forward surface.

[144] aka Bimini, two islands of Bahamas, E of S Florida and separated by Straits of Florida.

[145] Great Isaac Island (26°02'N., 79°05' W.) is near the NW extremity of Great Bahama Bank. It is a small, low barren islet extending to the ESE for 29 miles.

[146] Great Isaac Island is part of Great Bahama Bank that covers a large curved area some 330 m long with Andros on its E rim, separated from

Cuba on S by the Bahama Channel and from Florida on W and NW by Straits of Florida.

[147] To lay in wait.

[148] A four sided sail bent to a obliquely hanging yard that is hoisted and lowered with the sail with a foot larger than the head.

[149] Indicates basic principles of oceanography were understood and used by *Chasseur's* crew for navigation.

[150] Deficient in quantity or amount.

[151] Port town NE Virginia on Rappahannock River.

[152] A wooden container shaped like a pipe to fit into a cannon barrel holding grape or a cluster of small iron balls used as a cannon charge.

Appendix

"Sketch of the Gallant Achievements of the Heroic Captain Thomas Boyle, of the Privateer Brig *Chasseur*, of Baltimore on His Last Cruise in the British Channel, and Among the West India Islands, in the Winters of 1814 and 1815"

As recorded by George Coggeshall in *History of the American Privateers and Letters-of-Marque, during our War with England in the Years 1812, '13 and '14* published in 1856

(note: George Coggeshall was a highly respected contemporary of Tom Boyle who commanded several privateer schooners)

The *Chasseur* was a very formidable vessel, carrying sixteen long twelve pounders, and at the commencement of a cruise her crew probably amounted to one hundred men, including officers, seamen, and marines.

Here follows is a list of prizes made by this distinguished commander. This list is a portion (by no means all) of his captures, during a period of three months.

Sloop *Christiana*, of Kilkadee, Scotland, made a cartel of her, to disembarrass him from prisoners.

Brig *Reindeer*, of Aberdeen, from the Island of Lanzarote for London, with a cargo of wine and barrilla; manned her for the United States.

Schooner *Favorite*, also from Lanzarote, bound for London, with a similar cargo.

Brig *Marquis of Cornwallis*, from the same island, bound also for London. This vessel, being of small value, was made a cartel of, to get rid of prisoners.

English brig *Alert,* of Poole, from Newfoundland, with a cargo of timber, taken and destroyed.

Brig *Harmony,* of Aberdeen, from Newfoundland, bound for London, made a cartel of her, to be relieved from prisoners.

Ship *Carlbury*, of London, from Jamaica, with a very valuable cargo of cotton, cocoa, hides, indigo, etc., diverted her of two hundred and thirty-seven ceroon of indigo, and manned her for the United States. The goods taken from this prize were estimated at fifty thousand dollars.

Brig *Eclipse*, a valuable vessel of fourteen guns, sent to New York, at which place she arrived safe.

Brig *Commerce*, also a valuable vessel, laden with fish, ordered her to proceed to The United States.

Brig *Antelope*, carrying eight eighteen pound carronades, with a long tom, from Havana, laden with nine hundred boxes of sugar; she made no resistance, and was also sent to the United States.

British schooner *Fox* from Newfoundland, laden with fish for the Mediterranean, sent her to the United States.

Ship *James*, of London, with twelve guns and twenty men from the river La Plata, with hides, tallow, bark, furs, etc.

Brig *Atlantic*, also of London, with eight guns and fifteen men, from the river LaPlata, loaded with a similar cargo. The *James* and the *Atlantic* were in company, and were both captured and manned for the United States.

Ship *Theodore*, of Liverpool, with eight guns, from Marenham, with 1,660 bales of cotton, etc., etc.

Brig *Micus* of Liverpool, from Lisbon, with wool, fruit, and two bales of woolen goods.

Besides the vessels already enumerated there were others, whose names are not noticed in this list. The whole number of vessels captured by Captain, on this cruise, was eighteen, and many of them very valuable. Captain B. brought into port forty-three prisoners, and paroled one hundred and fifty. Had the *Chasseur* been a United States vessel, acting under orders to burn, sink and destroy all prizes, the loss to the enemy by this brig alone, would have exceeded a million and a half dollars. Although many of these prizes were probably re-captured, still the *Chasseur* must have made a very profitable cruise, for all who were concerned in this very fortunate privateer.

During Captain Boyle's cruise in the British Channel and around the coast of Great Britain, he had many hairbreadth escaped.

He was once so near a frigate as partially to exchange broadsides with her. At another time he was nearly surrounded by two frigates and two brigs-of-war, and in hauling off to avoid them, one of the frigates threw a show on board of his brig, and wounded three men; he, however, at length made his escape, and out-maneuvered and out-sailed them all.

At this period, it was the general custom for the British admirals on our coast to issue what the Americans called paper-blockades, declaring nearly the whole coast of North America in strict state of blockade, which, to have done effectually, would have required all the ships in the world. Several of these blockade-proclamations had recently been issued by Admiral Sir John Borlaise Warren and Sir Alexander Cocrane.

As a burlesque on these paper-blockades, Captain Boyle, while in the British Channel, issued the following proclamation, and sent it by a cartel to London, with a request to have it posted up at Loyd's Coffee House:

By Thomas Boyle, Esquire, Commander of the private armed brig Chasseur, etc., etc.

PROCLAMATION

Whereas it has become customary with the Admirals of Great Britain, commanding small forces on the coast of the United States, particularly with Sir John Borlaise Warren ( ) and Sir Alexander Cochrane,( ) to declare all the coast of the Said United States in a state of strict and rigorous blockade, without possessing the power to justify such a declaration, or stationing an adequate force to maintain said blockade.

I do, therefore, by virtue of the power and authority in vested (possessing sufficient force), declare all the ports, harbors, bays, creeks, rivers, inlets, outlets, islands and sea coast of the United Kingdom of Great Britain and Ireland in a state of strict and rigorous blockade.

And I do further declare, that I consider the force under my command adequate to maintain strictly, rigorously and effectually, the said blockade.

And I do hereby caution and forbid the ships and vessels of all and very nation, in amity and peace with the United States, from entering or attempting to enter, or from coming or attempting to come out of any of the said ports, harbors, bays, creeks, rivers inlets, outlets, islands, or sea coast, under any pretense whatsoever.

And that no person may plead ignorance of this, my proclamation, I have ordered the same to be made public in England.

Given under my hand on board the Chasseur, day and date as above.

Thomas Boyle

(By command of the commanding officer)
J. J. Stansbury, Secretary.

"Britannia needs no bulwark,
No towers along the steep;
Her march is o'er the mountain waves,
Her home is on the deep"

Arrival of the Privateer *Chasseur*

Captain Boyle arrived in Baltimore on the 15th of April, 1815 in the brig Chasseur, full of rich goods, spoils from the enemy, after a successful cruise among the Islands in the West Indies.

On entering the port, the Chasseur saluted Fort McHenry in a handsome style. Her brave captain and crew were welcomed by all classes of the community.

The Chasseur was a fine, large brig, and familiarly called "The Pride of Baltimore." She was indeed a fine specimen of naval architecture, and perhaps the most beautiful vessel that had floated on the ocean. She sat a light and buoyant on the water as a graceful swan, and it required but very little help of the imagination to feel that she was about to leave her watery element, and fly into the clear, blue sky.

Although this gallant vessel was so elegant and attractive to her friends, she carried dismay and terror to her enemies. During her last cruise, only seventeen days previous to her arrival in port, her heroic commander captured His Britannic Majesty's schooner St. Lawrence, mounting 15 carriage guns, with a crew of 75 men.

This action lasted but 15 minutes, when the Englishman surrendered his vessel, having been completely cut to pieces. Fifteen of his crew were killed, and 25 wounded; the Chasseur had but 5 men killed, and 8 wounded, and received little or no damage in her hull.

Her sails and rigging were somewhat injured, but were soon repaired, so that in a few hours she was ready for another action.
The Chasseur made several other prizes on this cruise, which have been recorded in their proper places.

On Captain Boyle's return home to Baltimore, he heard that a treaty of peace had been signed at Ghent, by the Ambassadors of the American and English governments. He then returned to the peaceful avocation of private life, to enjoy the esteem and applause of all those who had the honor of his acquaintance.

I cannot conclude my remarks on Captain Boyle's services to his state and county, without expressing a wish, that his name may be honored and cherished by every American heart, and I think he is richly entitled to a national monument, to perpetuate his memory to the latest generations.

The writer regrets that he never had the pleasure of a personal acquaintance with Captain Boyle; but from all he can hear of his character, to say that he was a dashing, brave man, could, in his case, be but common-place eulogy, for he was infinitely more than that idea expresses. He evidently possessed many of the elements of a great man, for in him were blended the impetuous bravery of a Murat with the prudence of a Wellington. He wisely judged when to attack the enemy, and when to retreat, with honor to himself, and to the flag under which he sailed.

The reader will please observe his daring bravery in cruising in the British Channel; and call to mind his many gallant victories, particularly when in command of the schooner Comet; in an action off Pernambuco, with a large Portuguese man-of-war-brig and three English merchantmen.

They were all well-armed and manned, notwithstanding which, Captain Boyle captured the three British vessels, and beat off the man-of-war.

The details of this battle may be found in the fourth chapter of this work.

In his last cruise in the Chasseur he also captured his Britannic Majesty's schooner St. Lawrence, of at least equal force with himself.

And then, reflect on his prudence in the management of his prizes.

He destroyed the dullest and poorest of them, and sent into port the best and most valuable, after having removed the specie, and all the most valuable articles into his own vessel, so as to secure a successful cruise to his owners, and to all others concerned in the enterprise.

As far as I can judge, he displayed in all his acts a sound judgment, beautifully blended with patriotic bravery.

Had this gentleman been a Commander in the United State Navy, his fame and deeds of valor would have been lauded throughout our great republic; but as he only commanded a privateer, who speaks for him? Or of such men as Diron, Chaplain, Murphy, Stafford, Wooster, and a host of others, who fought and bled in their country's cause.

It is not then narrow-minded prejudice not to award a just appreciation of the services of the gallant men who commanded privateers and letters-of-Marque during our severe struggle with England for an equal right to navigate the ocean, the great highway of nations. For it must certainly be conceded, that while condensing with the enemy at that period, the privateers and private armed vessels formed in fact a large portion of our navy, and were an indispensable auxiliary to it, as the militias and volunteers were to the United States Army.

—A History of American Privateers
by Edgar Stanton Maclay
Published New York 1899
Part Second
THE WAR OF 1812
Chapter V
CAPTAIN THOMAS BOYLE

(note: Edgar Stanton Maclay was highly respected historian of privateering during the War of 1812)

Appendix

Vessels noted in Logs of the voyages of Privateer *Comet*.

First Voyage:
  Lamprey
  Essex
  Active
  St. Franciscus
  Henry of Hull
  Madaira
  Hopewell
  Comet
  Swordfirsh
  Industry
  Resolution
  Nancy & Kate
  Lexis
  Swaggerer
  Dominica Packet
  James
  Yankee
  Surprise
  Newton
  Louis

Second Voyage:
  Donna Maria
  Wasa
  Bowes
  George
  Gambier
  Grand Sachem
  Calipso
  Swagger
  Dominica Packet
  James
  Yankee
  Surprise
  Newton
  Louis

Third Voyage
  Revenge
  Preciosa
  Fernandez
  Dei Biene
  Nuestra Senor de Corman
  Experiment
  Marlborough
  Lucetta
  Venus
  Carlscrona
  Messenger
  Hazard
  Industry
  Recruit
  Little Cherub
  Hannah
  Jackman
  Industry
  Enterprise
  Many
  Vigilant
  General Spooner
  Wasp
  Mars
  Endeavour
  General Pike

From Coggeshall's *History of American Privateers,* we can learn a few details of the first vessels to fit out from Baltimore and New York for privateering.

Baltimore:
- *Rossie*
- *Comet*
- *Dolphin*
- *Nonesuch*
- *Highflyer*
- *Globe*
- *America*
- *Bona*
- *Tom*
- *Sparrow*
- *Revenge*
- *Rolla*
- *Joseph & Mary*
- *Wasp*
- *Sarah Ann*
- *Liberty*
- *Hornet*

New York harbor:
- *Teazer*
- *Paul Jones*
- *Marengo*
- *Eagle*
- *Rosamond*
- *Benj. Franklin*
- *Black Joke*
- *Rover*
- *Orders of Council*
- *Saratoga*
- *United We Stand*
- *Divided We Fall*
- *Gov. Thompkins*
- *Retaliation*
- *Spitfire*
- *Gen. Armstrong*
- *Jack's Favorite*
- *Yorktown*
- *Tartar*
- *Holkar*
- *Anaconda*
- *Patriot*
- *Union*
- *Right of Search*
- *Bunker Hill*

Glossary

Sources:
A Dictionary of Sea Terms, A. Ansted
American Ship Models, V. R. Grimwood
Design Makes a Difference: Shipbuilding in Baltimore 1795–1835, Toni Ahrens
Dictionary of the Marine, William Falconer
International Maritime Dictionary, Rene de Kerchove
Lore of Ships, Tre Tryckare
Merriam Webster's Collegiate Dictionary
Nautical Word Book, Model Shipways
Paasch's Illustrated Marine Dictionary
Patterson's Illustrated Nautical Encyclopedia
Ships and Seamen of the American Revolution, Jack Coggins
The American Heritage Dictionary of the English Language
The USS Essex, Frances Robotti and James Vescovi
The Young Sea Officer's Sheet Anchor, Darcy Lever
Tidewater Triumph, Geoffrey M. Footner

A la *Chesapeake*: an invective against British for their actions of June 22, 1807 where HMS *Leopard* fired three salvos into *USS Chesapeake* took off English deserters then fired a broadside into the *Chesapeake* killing three and wounding 18 Americans. The affair grew large with the fury of thousands of impressments of Americans on this outrage of national honor.

Abaft: toward the stern.

Able seaman: the most senior of the ranks given to seaman in the united states navy in the nineteenth century. A man with no seafaring experience was rated as a landsman or boy if he was under eighteen on first entering the navy. After learning the basic skills (to hand, reef, and steer), he advanced to ordinary seaman. When he had learned to perform the above skills more proficiently and without supervision, he was promoted to able seaman. The process took about three years. The next step was to become a petty officer.

All hands to quarters: emergency call for all people aboard ship to turn out for orders.

Anchor: a large instrument of iron shaped like a hook having flukes or palms, and bills, shanks, arms, stock made of oak bolted together, hooped and farther secured by the nut, iron hoops, the eye for the ring, the ring and the crown of the anchor.

for a brig of ca. 1800 with a keel of 75 ft., 27 ft. Beam and 11 1/2 ft depth of hold, the anchors and cables are as follows:

bower (3): 1500 lbs.

stream anchor: 600 lbs

kedge: 300 lbs.

grapnel: 28 lbs.

cables: hemp cables should be one inch in circumference for each foot of the ship's beam.

Articles of War: a list of 35 stipulations as to conduct within the Royal Navy establishment dating from 1757. These were read publicly at the commissioning of new ships, at least once a month, usually when church was rigged on Sunday, when an offender's punishment warrant was read to the ship's company and at timely intervals by the captain to the ship's company. In the British navy during the age of sail, flogging was the most common of all punishments. Warrant punishments were "read" publicly while the offender stood to attention in front of the formally mustered ship's company. The articles of war on board a Royal Navy ship matched the gravity of holy writ. It served as the law practiced on his majesty's ships. The articles were originally established in the 1650s, amended in 1749 and again in 1757. The basic disciplinary rules that governed the Royal Navy. Every other Sunday at sea, the captain of a Royal Navy ship was required to read aloud the articles of war to his crew so that no one could claim ignorance through illiteracy. On the other Sundays, a church service was conducted.

Athwart: to lie across the line of movement of a vessel.

Bale cotton: any of various plants or shrubs of the genus *gossypium*, cultivated in warm climates for the fiber surrounding their seeds; a major trade commodity of West Indies.

Glossary

Beating to windward: making progress against the direction of the wind when sailing on the wind or close-hauled.

Bend: to fasten; a knot that joins a rope to a rope or another object.

Bends; bent wood: the thick planks in a ship's side; the wales.

Bentick shroud: a shroud designed to take the strain of the futtock shrouds on the fore and mainmast by joining them at an iron ring that is connected to a heavy shroud that leads down by tackle to an eyebolt in the deck aft of the mast.

Bermuda Sloop: prototype of early form of west indies craft that evolved from Jamaica sloop that became popular when built in Bermuda where there was sufficient cedar timber. For the island trade, smuggling and piratical needs these were small fast weatherly vessels hiding in cays and mangrove swamps. By 1750 the name "Jamaica Sloop" had become the "Bermuda Sloop"; a single masted, fore-and-aft rigged sailing vessel with a short standing bowsprit or none at all and a single headsail set from the forestay.

Best bower & small bower: these are anchors stowed in the farthest forward, or near the bows.

Between wind and water: a descriptive term for that part of a ship which lies above the waterline and the top of the hull.

Bill of lading: a document listing and acknowledging receipt of goods for shipment.

Block and tackle: before the middle of the nineteenth century, heavy lifting, pulling, and hauling was done by the brute strength of the crew. In order to assist, ropes were run through combinations of wooden pulleys, called blocks. Such a set was called a block and tackle providing considerable mechanical advantage.

Boarding netting: heavy rope netting placed above waterline for climbing the sides of the ship.

Bobstays: the chains or ropes leading from the underneath outboard end of the bowsprit to the stem where they are secured, and by which the bowsprit is held down and prevented from jumping.

Bore away, bore up: to proceed or advance steadily or laboriously.

Bower: the heaviest of a ship's anchors, carried at the bow; aka bower anchor.

Bowsprit shrouds: the ropes leading from the side of the bowsprit cap back to the bows of the vessel where they are set up, and which stay the bowsprit sideways.

Box hauling: a method of waring or turning a ship from the wind.

Braces: a rope by which a yard is swung and secured on a square-rigged ship.

Brailed up: a line used to furl loose-footed sail; to gather in a sail with brails.

Breechings of guns: a rope securing the breech of a cannon to the side of a ship to control recoil and to control cannon in heavy weather.

Brig: a two masted sailing ship, square rigged on both masts, carrying two or more headsails and a quadrilateral gaff sail or spanker aft on the mizzen mast. The *Chasseur* was re-rigged as a brig at New York for her last voyage. A small vessel with two masts carrying square rigged sails. A brig was generally larger than a schooner but smaller than a ship.

Broadside: the side of a ship above the water line; all the guns on one side of a warship; their simultaneous discharge; firing of all the guns on one side of a ship simultaneously for maximum shock effect.

Brooming: to sweep with a broom.

Canister: a cylindrical metal container, much like a modern soup can, filled with iron or lead balls or scrap iron, fired from a cannon, it acted like a huge shotgun.

Carronade: a short, light muzzle-loading gun that fired a heavy round shot at a limited range; from the Carron iron works, Carron, Scotland. Nicked named "smashers" in Royal Navy for damage they could do.

Cartel vessel: normally an unarmed merchant ship owned or leased by the government and used to transport exchanged or paroled prisoners of war, under a flag of truce, from their place of confinement to a friendly port.

Catharpins or cat harpin: lengths of rope used for binding the shrouds abreast of the topsail yards, in order that those yards may be braced up as sharp as possible.

Caulk: to make watertight a seam in planking, by forcing in strips of tarred rope fibers. Seams on deck planking were then "played" by the application of hot pitch.

Ceroon: a bale or package covered with hide or with wood bound with hide as packaging to ship indigo.

Chapelling: a ship is said to build a chapel, when by neglect in light winds she turns round so as to bring the wind on the same part which it was before she moved.

Chase: the vessel being chased by a privateer.

Clear for action: to go through the list necessary to prepare vessel for combat. A warship preparing for battle took a number of steps to increase fighting efficiency, such as extinguishing all flames and fires, laying out small arms, and spreading sand on the decks to give the gun crews better traction. When these and other steps had been completed, the ship was said to be "cleared for action." A well-trained crew could clear for action in about ten minutes.

Close-hauled: sailing close to the wind.

Cocoa: a powder made from cacao seeds after they have been roasted, ground, and freed from their fatty oil; a major trade commodity of West Indies.

Coffee: any of several trees of the genus *coffea*, native to eastern Asia and Africa, bearing berries containing beans used in the preparation of a beverage; especially, *c. Arabica*, the chief commercial source of these beans.

Come about: to bring a ship into the wind and onto another tack.

Come up into the wind: to turn a ship so that the wind is right ahead, either to lose way preparatory to stopping or anchoring, or to go about on another tack.

Commodore: the courtesy title given to a captain commanding a squadron of several ships.

Convoy: ships sailing together under escort of an armed ship.

Cordage: a naval term that collectively encompasses all the different types of rope and line that would be carried in or on a ship.

Crank: a description of a vessel that heels too easily in a wind; liable to capsize, unstable.

Cutter: a ship's boat powered by oars and used for transporting stores or passengers.

Drag of the keel: a characteristic of Baltimore schooners, pilot-boat built where the difference between the depth of the bow and that of the deeper stern is considerable.

En fluyt: this a Dutch vessel type designed and used only for cargo carrying.

Fighting sail: for ease of handling, with a minimum of men aloft, a ship going into action often reduced her canvas to topsails, spanker, and jib. Courses were usually clewed up. Topgallants were sometimes only loosely furled or the yards were lowered to the caps with the sails loose.

Filled away: to set sails to catch wind thereby moving vessel.

Fishing as in mast or spar: to or reunite a spar by bolting pieces of plank over the fish or pieces.

Flag of truce vessel: a vessel carrying papers or flag indicating to others that the ship and its crew are noncombatants.

Floated: when vessel previously aground floats free.

Foremast jack: a common sailor.

Foretop: a platform located approximately one third of the way up the forward-most mast in a vessel with two or more masts. It was used as a foundation for mounting and spreading rigging and for supporting the other parts of the mast above it. In a three masted ship, the other masts (mainmast and mizzenmast) would have similar tops and be named appropriately. In a warship, seamen and marines armed with muskets, were stationed in the tops to shoot down on the enemy. The dress uniform of the marines includes a rope and knot pattern on the top of the hat so that sharp shooters can differentiate between friend and foe from the tops of the vessel.

Frigate: a class of ship employed in almost all navies during the sailing era, a frigate carried three square-rigged masts and was armed with between thirty and forty-nine guns and was known for speed. Frigates were principally used for scouting, escorting convoys, and commerce raiding and were powerful to overwhelm smaller warships.

Fustic: yellow dyestuff from tropical American tree *chlorohora tinctoria*. Trade item of the West Indies.

Futtock shrouds: short shrouds leading from the futtock band to the futtock plates; the former is a band near the top of a lower mast; the latter lie across the top of a lower mast, and to them are secured the deadeyes of the topmast rigging.

Gaff: a spar used to extend the top edge of a fore-and-aft sail.

Gammoning: in order to keep the bowsprit down firm, and to resist the great force of the stays which support the masts forwards, it is confined to its situation by the gammoning, bobstays and shrouds. The gammonings is a rope passed with 8, 10 or 12 turns over the bowsprit, and through a hole in the cutwater. The gammoning is then hove well taught and then sufficiently nippered with spun-yarn to the standing part.

Grog: an allowance of 90 proof rum, mixed with water, issued daily, on a warship, to all hands eighteen years or older. It was doled out just prior to the noonday meal. Whiskey was sometimes substituted for rum. If he wished, a non-drinker could receive a money allowance instead of grog.

Hail, hailed: to call out to another ship.

Hammock netting: a topside feature of a ship either wood or iron where hammocks were place prior to action to provide cover for deck crew and reduce to effect of flying splinters, otherwise a place to air and dry bedding.

Handed; to hand or to furl; furling; making fast the sails to the yards by the gaskets.

Hardtack: also called ship's bread or ship's biscuit. Hardtack resembled a large, thick cracker (about four by four inches) and consisted of flour, salt, and yeast mixed with a minimum of water. Long slow baking was used to preserve the biscuit. By the time it was eaten, a biscuit could be rock hard and infested with weevils. Sailors would frequently rap their biscuits on a hard surface to dislodge the larva and beetles.

Hauled off: to change the course of a ship.

Haulyard: also halliard, a rope used to raise or lower a sail, flag or yard.

Headsails: jibs and staysails set between the bowsprit and the foremost mast.

Hoggsheads, hogsshead: any of various units of volume or capacity ranging from 62.5 to 140 gallons especially a unit of capacity used in liquid measure in the united states equal to 63 gallons.

Hove about: past tense of to heave; to raise an anchor; to pull on or haul a rope; to come to be in a specified position; to raise or seemingly raise into view, as a ship; to turn a sailing ship so that its bow heads into the wind as by way of meeting a storm.

Hulk: an old and otherwise useless ship, usually a former warship, that had been stripped of all masts, rigging, stores and guns. These vessels or hulks were then frequently used as warehouses, barracks, and prisons and with lower mast left in place and rigged with heavy tackle, the vessel could be used as a sheer hulk to lift masts out of vessels undergoing refitting or repair.

Hung fire, hang fire: when a weapon does not fire immediately.

Impress: the term used in Great Britain to describe the lawful process by which British seamen were drafted into the Royal Navy when manpower needs were great and volunteers few. Organized "press gangs" swept through British seaports to secure sailors. At sea, captains could impress sailors from British merchant ships, as long as a bare minimum of hands were left to sail the vessel to port.

In ballast: a quantity of iron, stone, or gravel etc placed in the hold to give a ship proper stability, when she has no cargo, or but a small quantity of goods.

Indigo: a blue vat dye obtained from indigo plants; a plant that yields indigo; especially any of genus *indigofera* of leguminous herbs; in this usage, seroma is a liquid form of processed plant material. (See Seroma entry.)

Junk: old cordage, rope, reused for gaskets, oakum, and mats.

Keckling: old rope passed around the cable at short distances.

Kedge: a light anchor used for warping a vessel.

Ketch: a two masted fore-and-aft rigged sailing vessel with a mizzen mast stepped aft of a taller mainmast but forward of the rudder.

Langrage: a mixture of metal scrap, such as bolts, nails and iron bars, sewn into a sausage-like bag of canvas and fired from a cannon. Cheap and effective, langrage was devastating when fired against mast, sails, rigging and any sailor unlucky enough to get in the way.

Lazaretto: a cruiser striped and housed over to be used as a hospital ship for sailors with contagious diseases.

League: a distance measure of three statute miles.

Leeward: being in or facing the direction toward which the wind is blowing, opposite to windward.

Letter of Marque trader: a vessel operating under the legality of a Letter of Marque (being a Man of Marque). A government issued Letter of Marque and reprisal gave license to a ship's captain to engage in warlike acts in self defense. Letter of Marque traders could seek out targets of opportunity (pronounced "letter of mark").

Letter of Marque: Webster's Collegiate Dictionary defines it as: "written authority granted to a private person by a government to seize the subjects of a foreign state or their goods: specifically: a license granted to a private person to fit out an armed ship to plunder the enemy; a document issued by a nation allowing a private citizen to seize citizens or goods of another nation; a document issued by a nation allowing a private citizen to equip a ship with arms in order to attack enemy ships; also called 'Letter of Marque and Reprisal.'"

Lignum vita: a tropical American tree *gualacum officinale* having evergreen leaves and heavy durable resinous wood; used in ship construction due to its strength. Trade item of west indies.

Liner: short for "ship of the line."

Luffed up: the act of sailing closer into the wind; to steer a sailing ship nearer into the wind especially with the sails flapping.

Man-of-war: a warship of whatever size owned and operated by a legitimate government.

Marestier: a French marine engineer and naval architect sent to America to study and report on steamboats and who measured and drew pilot schooners under construction at Fells Point in the 1820's.

Mast sprung: the warping, bending, or cracking such as that caused by excessive force applied to the mast of a ship. With time and exposure masts dried out becoming brittle and prone to breakage.

Merchantman: a privately owned ship used for the carrying of cargo and/or passengers.

Meridian: noon.

Molasses: any of various thick syrups produced in refining sugar; major trade commodity of West Indies.

Nippers: plaitings selvagees used to bind a cable to a revolving rope messenger.

Off shore: moving or directed away from the shore; at a distance from the shore.

Officers: commissioned, warrant and petty; including master boatswain, gunner, coxswain, master-at-arms, carpenter, sailmaker, midshipmen.

Paroled prisoner: the release of a prisoner before his term has expired on condition of good behavior.

Pipe: a wine cask having a capacity of 126 gallons.

Pirate: one who robs at sea or plunders the land from the sea without commission from a sovereign nation.

Private armed vessel: a descriptive definition of a privateer.

Privateer: a ship privately owned and manned but authorized by a government during wartime to attack and capture enemy vessels. Norman G. Rukert writes in *The Fells Point Story*: "A privateer was a privately-owned vessel, armed and manned at her owner's expense for the purpose of capturing enemy merchant craft in time of war. International law required that she have a commission, or Letter-of-Marque, from her government, otherwise she would be considered a pirate. To obtain a Letter-of-Marque a vessel had to be bonded to the government to satisfy any claims that might arise from illegal captures; two bonds were needed for each privateer. Theoretically, the privateer had no right to her prizes until they were condemned by due process of law, but as the privateer could destroy vessels at sea, this was a mere formality." The owner, officers and crew held shares in the privateering enterprises. A privately owned armed vessel that operated in time of war against the enemy principally against the enemy's merchant trade. The term privateer derived from combining "private" and "volunteer." The activities of a privateer were made legal by a document called a Letter of Marque and Reprisal," issued by the government. Without this document, a privateer could be defined as a pirate and the entire crew hanged, if captured. America made great use of privateers during the Revolutionary War and the War of 1812 as a way of augmenting its small navy at little expense.

Prize master: officer of privateer appointed by captain to take a prize vessel to the u.s. Or a friendly port using a prize crew.

Prize ship: ship taken by privateer from which cargo is removed or the vessel is sailed to a neutral port for admiralty court disposition. Once a specifically designated court verified that the prize had been legitimately captured, it would be sold and the proceeds divided among the victorious crew.

Prize ticket: the document given by a captain of a privateer stating the entitlement of each man aboard to the proceeds of prizes taken during a voyage of a privateer.

Protection: to ward off possible impressment, many American sailors carried documents issued by United States magistrates and consuls to prove their true nationality. Such a document was called a protection. Many Royal Navy officers, in their zeal to impress any likely looking sailor, ignored these documents, claiming that they were bogus. In truth many were.

Pudding the rings: the rings of the anchors are well parceled with tarred canvas, and then wrapped round with twice-laid stuff (rope) this is called "puddening the anchor."

Puncheon: a large cask of varying capacity, cask with a capacity of 84 us gallons.

Purchase: a mechanical appliance to obtain an increase in power; a purchase is formed by ropes and blocks (tackle).

Quick roller: a vessel unstable in any sea.

Quick-way: fast moving or swift movement of one vessel in relationship to another.

Rake: to position one's vessel across another vessel's bow or stern so that its fire can sweep the enemy's decks. Position of masts of a vessel off vertical.

Rattling: to secure rattlines to shrouds, usually "rattling down."

Razee: when major top-side elements are removed from a ship of the line such as spar deck and battery, the vessel becomes a heavy frigate, a razee.

Reef: when the wind increased significantly, a ship had to reduce the area of exposed sail or risk damage to masts and rigging. To do this the sails were reefed. Most large square sails were equipped with horizontal rows of short lengths of rope called reef points. To take a reef in a sail, the sail was hauled part way up to its yard and the reef points tied together over the top of the yard. This action could reduce the amount of exposed sail by 25 to 75 percent, depending on which row of reef points were used.

Rounded to; rounding: made round; shaped in a circle.

Schooner: a ship with two or more masts, all of which are fore-and-aft rigged, the mainmast being abaft of and taller than the fore mast.

Scupper: opening in side of ship at deck level to allow water to run off.

Seroma: this is a medical term used to describe the localized Accumulation of fluid in a body in relation to a wound or incision. In the context of this narrative it is a container in the fermentation process and settling out of the blue sludge from indigo mash including the enzyme formation (reaction) of indigo to oxygen and then the subsequent shipment of the liquid dye to fabric mills.

Shackle bolt: metal fastener which secures chain cable or shrouds to ships side by means of a forelock and a bolt.

Sheers: the upward curve or the amount of upward curve, of the longitudinal lines of a ship's hull as viewed from the side.

Sheired close: a turn, deviation, or change in a course as of a ship; to go in and out, and not in a direct course.

Sheired off: to swerve or deviate from a course.

Shrouds: stays running from the masthead to the ship's side and set up by deadeyes.

Signal numbers: each telegraph signal sent or received had a number that was recorded, and used again as appropriate for the same message.

Slings and straps: short ropes or chains used to hang the yards to the mast, hence, the middle part of the yard, between such gear; to fit or furnish with a strap of strop; a piece of rope or metal passing around a block, deadeye, or spar.

Sloop of war: a small warship with guns on only one deck.

Slops: articles of clothing and bedding issued to sailors from a ship's stores.

Sounding: a measured depth of water.

Splinter nets: movable rope nets to protect the crew from flying splinters.

Spring: a rope made fast to the cable at the bow, and taken in abaft, in order to expose the ship's side to any direction. When at anchor, a sailing ship points into the wind like a weather vane. To turn the ship, a line was run from the capstan out through some opening near the stern and then made fast to the anchor line as near to the anchor as possible. This line was called a spring. By hauling in on the spring, the ship could be turned toward whatever side the spring tended in spite of the wind.

Square tuck/flat transom: the part of a ship's hull under the stern where the ends of the bottom planks come together.

Standing: to take or hold a particular course or direction; to steer; a ship standing to windward.

Steering sails: see sails listed under fighting sails.

Steeve: the angle of the bowsprit above the horizontal.

Stern chaser: long range canon placed at stern of a vessel.

Stiving: the bowsprit projects over the stem: and rises upwards in a sloping direction, which is termed stiving.

Stream anchor: used to bring the ship up or to steady a ship when she comes to a temporary mooring.

Studding sail: a narrow rectangular sail set from extensions of the yards of square-rigged ships.

Sugar: cane sugar processed in islands and shipped in casks; major trade commodity of west indies; a tall grass *saccharum officinarum*, native to the east indies, having thick, tough stems that are one of the chief commercial sources of sugar.

Supercargo: an officer on board a merchant ship who has charge of the cargo and its sale and purchase.

Supernumerary: a person in excess of the regular, necessary, or usual number aboard a ship.

Glossary

Swayed up: to swing into position, as a mast or a yard using powder of the ships movement as it lay at anchor.

Sweeping: to clean or clear the surface of with a pass of a broom or brush.

Tacked again and weathered: to change course from being obliquely opposed to the direction of the wind by putting down the helm.

Tacked ship: to bring a vessel into the wind in order to change tack; the position of a vessel relative to the trim of its sails.

Tackle: an arrangement of ropes and pulleys for hoisting or pulling heavy objects.

Taffrail: the rail around the stern of a vessel.

Telegraph: a visual signaling system made up of flags used between ships and/or shore installations, a visual signal of flags hoisted on haliyards for visibility.

Tierces: a former measure of liquid capacity, equal to a third of a pipe or 42 gallons.

To bowse: to haul upon.

To broach to: flying up in the wind so as to bring it on the other side, when blowing fresh.

To quarters: ship board command to prepare for battle.

Topinlift, toppinglift: a purchase for topping (lifting) a boom and sustaining the weigh of the after-end of the same.

Triced up: to hoist and secure (a sail for example); to lash.

Unshipped: to become loose or undone.

Upon a wind: to move with a prevailing wind.

Veer; veered: to change the direction of a ship by turning away from the direction of the wind; to wear ship.

Waist: the middle part of the deck of a ship between the forecastle and the quarter-deck or poop deck.

Waring; wearing: to change to an opposite tack by turning the stern to the wind.

Warping: to move a vessel by hauling on a line that is fastened to or around a piling, anchor, or pier.

Weather beam: when wind comes across the side of the ship.

Weather bow: that side of the ship bow facing into the weather (wind).

Weather gauge: a position on windward side of enemy ship or fleet

Weather quarter: of or pertaining to the side of a ship toward the wind; windward.

Weathered away: to pass to windward of, despite bad weather.

Woolding: the act of winding a piece of rope about a mast or yard, to support it in a place where it may have been fished or scarfed, or when it is composed of several pieces united into one solid also the rope employed in this service.

Wore ship: past tense of to wear or to turn, as a ship.

Yawed off: to deviate from the intended course; to move unsteadily.

Zebec: a small three-masted Mediterranean vessel with both square and triangular sails.

Sources

Books

Admiral George Cockburn Papers. Washington, D.C.: Manuscripts Division, Library of Congress.

Ahrens, Toni. *Design Makes a Difference: Shipbuilding in Baltimore 1795-1835*. Bowie, MD: Heritage Books Inc., 1998.

Ansted, A. *A Dictionary of Sea Terms*. Glasgow: Brown and Son and Ferguson Ltd., 1933.

Chapelle, Howard I. *The History of American Sailing Ships*. New York: Bonanza Books. 1935.

Chapelle, Howard I. *The History of The American Sailing Navy*. New York: Bonanza Books, 1949.

Chapelle, Howard Irving. *The Baltimore Clipper*. New York: Dover Publications, 1930.

Coggeshall, George. *History of American Privateers and Letters of Marque*. New York: 1856.

Cooper, James Fenimore. *Ned Myers, or a Life before the Mast*. New York: Stringer & Townsend, 1854.

Cranwell, John P. & William B. Crane, *Men of Marque*, New York: W.W. Norton & Co., 1940

Culver. Henry B. *The Book of Old Ships*, Garden City, NY: Garden Publishing Co., 1935.

Footner, Geoffrey M. *Tidewater Triumph*. Cambridge, MD: Tidewater Publishers, 1998.

Garitee, Jerome R. *The Republic's Private Navy*. Middletown, CT: Wesleyan University Press, 1977.

Grimwood, V. R. *American Ship Models and How to Build Them*. New York: WW Norton & Co., Inc., 1942.

Hopkins, Fred W. Jr. *Tom Boyle: Master Privateer*. Cambridge, MD: Tidewater Publishers, 1976.

De Kerchove, Rene. *International Maritime Dictionary*. Toronto, New York and Longdon: D. VanNostrand Co., 1948.

Laing, Alexander. *American Sail: A Pictorial History*. New York: Bonanza Book, 1969.

Laing, Alexander. *Seafaring America*. New York: American Heritage, 1974.

Landstrom, Bjorn. *The Ship: An Illustrated History*. New York: Doubleday, 1961.
Lever, Darcy. *The Young Sea Officer's Sheet Anchor*. London: 1819.
Maclay, Edgar Stanton. *A History of American Privateers*. New York: 1899.
Marryat, Captain Frederick. *Frank Mildmay or, The Naval Officer*. A project for Arthur's Classic Novels. ETexts was prepared from borrowed Athelstane E-Texts at http://athelstane.co.uk/. XHTML markup Arthur Wendover, mail@arthurwendover.com, November 1, 2002. This is the etext version of the book, *Frank Mildmay by Captain Maryat*, taken from the original etext frkmld10.txt. Arthurs' Classic Novels.
Men, Ships and the Sea. Washington, D.C.: National Geographic Society, 1962.
Nautical Word Book: Being Definitions of Common Sea Terms of Yesterday & Less Common Ones of Today. Bogota, NJ: Model Shipways, 1961.
Paasch, Captain H. *Paasch's Illustrated Marine Dictionary*. New York: Lyons & Burford, 1885.
Patterson's Ilustrated Nautical Encyclopedia, 1901
Robotti, Frances, and James Vescovi. *The USS* Essex *and the Birth of the American Navy*. Holbrook, MA: Adams Media Corp., 1999.
Rukert, Norman G. *The Fells Point Story*. Baltimore: Bodine & Associates, 1976.
Sailing Directions (Enroute) Carribbean Sea. Vol. 1 (Pub. 147). Annapolis, MD: Lighthouse Press, 2004.
Shomette, Donald. *Flotilla Battle for the Patuxent*. Solomons, MD: Calvert Marine Museum Press, 1981.
Svensson, Sam. *Sails Through the Centuries*. New York: 1965.
The American Heritage Dictionary of the English Language.
Tryckare, Tre. *The Lore of Ships*. New York: Holt, Rinehart and Winston, 1963.
Websters New Geographical Dictionary, G. & C. Merriam Co.

Articles

"An Act concerning Letters of Marque, Prizes, and Prize Goods."

"Privateering in the War of 1812."

"The *Comet's* Cruise, by Thomas Boyle for the *Baltimore Patriot*." *Republican Star* (Easton, MD), April 12, 1814.

HMS St. Lawrence *Log Book between the 1st Oct. 1813 and the 12th October 1814.*

Dudley, William S., Editor, and Michael J. Crawford, Associate Editor. *The Naval War of 1812: A Documentary History.* (3 vols.) Vol. I, 1812. Washington: Naval Historical Center, Department of the Navy, 1985.

Hoyte, William D., Jr. "Logs and Papers of Baltimore Privateers, 1812-15." *Maryland Historical Magazine*, Vol. 34, 1939.

Logs of British Ships in the Patuxent (H.M.S. *St. Lawrence*), *Chronicles of St. Mary's,* Vol. 11, No. 12, 12/1963 and Vol. 13, No. 4, 4/1965.

Niles' Weekly Register, No. 7 of Vol. VIII, Saturday, April 15, 1815.

Niles' Weekly Register, No. 4 of Vol. VIII, Saturday, March 23, 1815.

White, Frank F. Jr. (ed.), "The *Comet* Harasses the British." *Maryland Historical Magazine*, Vol. 53, Number 4, December, 1958.

Index

----, Peter, 79
Abbaco, 71
Aberdeen, 19, 117
Active, 9, 123
Adams, Daniel, 48
Addison, Overton, 50
Adelphi, 19, 103
Admiral Laforey, 29, 33
Adventure, 70, 102, 104
Ahrens, Toni, 5
Alert, 104, 117
Alexis, 20, 103
Altwalla Rock, 71
Amelia Island, 28, 81
America, 124
Amicus, 104
Anaconda, 36, 42–43, 124
Anderson, William, 10–11
Anegada Channel, 23
Angola, 21
Anguella, 33
Anguilla, 32
Ann Maria, 104
Antelope, 104, 118
Antigua, 33
Antiqua, 32
Arenatta Bay, 73
Argus, 9, 24
Aruba, 72
Asp, 36–37
Atlantic, 104, 118
Atlas, xi, 36–37, 39–43, 79, 98
Austen, Purnel, 12
Aveline, Thomas, 91
Badger, Elijah, 50
Bahia, 19, 21
Bainbridge, William, 7

Baker, Nicholas, 11
Ball
  C., 91
  John, 49
  Mr., 20
Baltimore Clipper, vii, viii
Baltimore Flyer, viii
Baltimore, Maryland, vii–x, 22, 24–26, 34, 97, 100, 102–104, 117, 120–121, 124
Baltimore Patriot, newspaper, 26
Baney, John, 31
Barbados, 28, 33, 60, 64–66
Barker, John B,, 48
Barnes, John, 48
Barney, Joshua, 34
Barrossa, 67, 99, 102
Bartlett, William, 19
Basse-Terre, 24
Beaufort, North Carolina, 13, 104
Belvidera, 9
Benj. Franklin, 124
Benson, John, 29
Benta, 71
Bequia, 62
Berg, John, v
Bermuda, xi, 28, 33, 35, 87, 96
Berry, John, 50
Betten, John, 91
Bettys, Henry, 50
Bimini, 81
Bird, Jerome, v
Black, Edward, 31
Black Joke, 124
Blackware, Chat., 91
Bladensburg, 26
Blenkinshop, John, 7

Blockade, by Tom Boyle in Britain and Ireland, 97
Blockades, American ports, 1–2
Blockades of American ports, 13–14, 24, 34
"Blucher", 55
Bona, 124
Bond, William Cranch, 5
Bootman, John, 50
Boston, 12, 14, 25, 27, 84
Bowes, 17–18, 103, 123
Boyle
  Mary (Gross), x
  Thomas, 15–16
  Tom, viii, x–xii, 5, 22–27, 33, 45, 48, 53–54, 57, 86, 89, 97, 99–104, 117–122
Bradford, ----, 36
Brazil, 7, 13
Brenner, Lucy, 11
Bridgetown, 60–61
Briggs, Benjamin, 50
Bristol, 21, 37
Britannia, 104
Broke, P.B.V., 14
Brook Haven, Ireland, 81
Brown
  Benjamin, 50
  George, 49
  Hugh, 91
  John, 48
  John H., 49
Buffalo, New York, 14
Bullock, Joseph, 48
Bunker Hill, 124
Burk, Jacob, 48, 100
Byng, Henry Dilkes, 36
Cadiz, 12, 27, 81
Cadle, Thomas, 10
Cale, Charles, 90
Calipso, 19, 123
Callehe, 90–91
Campeache, 75

Cape Antonio, 75–76
Cape Coruntes, 75
Cape Cruz, 73
Cape Henry, 9, 15, 24, 27, 85
Cape Liberoon, 72
Cape Verde, 10
Carey, Edward, 10
Carlbury, 105, 117
Carlescrona, 28
Carley, Rogers, 36
Carlscrona, 123
Carpenter
  James, 50
  John, 100
Carrere, John, x
Carthagena, 71
Caskey, Roberts, 50
Castro, 64
Cathell, 54
  Clement, 26, 103
  H. P., 85–86
  Lt., 19, 23
  Mr., 20–21
  William, 10
Cellis, Thomas, 50
Charleston, 14, 28, 102, 105
Chase
  B., 48
  Comet, 51
  Thorndike, 5
Chasseur, viii–xi, 45–47, 53, 56–57, 80, 85–86, 88–89, 97–102, 104, 117–118, 120–121
Cherub, 24
Chesapeake, 14, 25
Chesapeake Bay, vii–viii, 11, 14, 25, 84, 98, 102
  blockaded, 34–35
Chesapeake Bay Flotilla, 34
Chivers, Capt., 37
Christian, Martin, 91
Christiana, 105, 117
Christie, Mr., 79, 98

Clark, Peter, 49, 82, 100
Cochrane
  Lt., 96
  Sir Alexander, 87
Cockburn, Sir George, 14, 34–36, 42, 88
Cockchafer, 35, 42
Cocrane, Sir Alexander, 119
Coffin, Cabil, 48
Coggeshall, 37
  George, 117, 124
Coles, Charles, 91
Collins, Thomas, 50
Comet, viii–xi, 5, 9–12, 15, 20–21, 23, 25–26, 28, 32–33, 86, 103, 121, 123–124
Comet, celestial, 5
Commerce, 105, 118
Conflict, 35, 42
Congress, 9
Conrad, Dennis, v
Constitution, 7–8, 11, 13
Contest, 36
Convoy, 77, 82
Cook, William, 91
Cordelia, x
Corruna, 105
Corunna, 69
Cottom, Richard, v
Cousins, John, 91
Coward, Thomas, 48
Crane, xi
  William Bowers, 103
Cranwell, xi
  John Philips, 103
Crawford, Mike, v
Crea, Hugh, 100
Creek War, 26
Crocker, Capt., 70
Crockner, Edward, 49
Crooker, Charles, 91
Cuba, 73, 88
Culver, Henry B., 56

Curacao, 68
Curacoa, 32–33
Curry, Lt., 36–37
Davis
  Otho H., 48
  Thomas, 49, 79, 100
Davy, Sir Humphry, 55
Decatur, Stephen, 7
Dei Biene, 27, 123
Delaware River, blockaded, 34
Demarara, 20–21
Demologos Fulton, 55
Dempster, Capt., 69
Dent, John, 19
Detroit, Michigan, 7, 14
Dew, Edward, 48
Di???, Thomas, 49
Diamond Point, 64
Dickson, William, 50
Dieter, 54
  John, 48, 85–86, 99, 104
Dilke, Charles, 87
Divided We Fall, 124
Dix, Edward, 87
Dog Keys, 23
Dolphin, 124
Dolphin, Francis, 50
Dominica Packet, 103, 123
  Liverpool, 21
Dongall, H. M., 50
Donna Maria, 15, 123
Drake's Bay, 31
Dryden, James, 10
Dudley, William, ix
Duff, Hugh, 49
Duffie, Barnard, 50
Dungan, Abil S., 48
Duvall, William H., 48
Eagle, 124
Eclipse, 62, 105, 118
Elba, 26
Eldridge, Matthew, 49
Eliza Ross, 84

Elizabeth, 61, 105
Endeavor, 32–33, 103, 123
Endymion, 63
Enterprise, 29
Enterprize, 33, 103, 123
Essex, 9, 24, 42, 123
Expedition, x
Experiment, 27, 33, 103, 123
Farrill, George, 50
Fast Sailing Schooner, viii
Favourite, 105, 117
Fells Point, Maryland, vii, ix, 5, 86
Fernandez, 27, 123
Fernando de Norohna, 21
Firth, Capt., 37
Fisher, G., 91
Fitzgerald, Edward, 49
Fitzherbert, Andrew, 87
Flaugergues, Pierre-Giulles-Antoine Honore, 5
Footner, Geoffrey, v
Fort McHenry, v, 9, 13, 26, 34, 102, 120
Fort Niagara, 14
Fort Richmond, 56
Fort Royal, 82
Fort Royal Bay, 63–64
Foster
  Augustus John, 6
  Mr., 39
  W., 49
Fox, 35, 42, 105, 118
Frame, John, 51
Francis, Thomas, 49
Frederick, John, 49
Fredericksburg, 85
Freeman, Christopher, v
Frizill, John, 49
Frolic, 7
Fulton, Robert, 55
Galatea, 104
Gambier, 18, 123
Gamble, 18

Gantz, A. Jr., 48
Gausaloa, Joseph, 49
Gen. Armstrong, 124
General Pike, 123
General Spooner, 31, 33, 103, 123
General Wale, 32–33, 103
George, 18, 123
George, Christopher, v
Georgetown, 74
Georgia, 14
Gibbs, Samuel (Wm), 50
Gibraltar, 19, 21
Gillit, Joseph, 48
Gilpin, Mr., 20
Gleeson, John, 50
Globe, 124
Glouster (Gloucester), Mass., 11
Gordon
  Charles, 25
  James Edward, xi, 79–80, 87, 90–98, 100–102
  Ruben G., 51
Goree, 87, 96
Gotteburg, 27
Gould, Obediah B., 49
Gov. Thompkins, 124
Graham, Thomas, 49
Granada, 68
Granadillos Island, 68
Grand Cayman Island, 74
Grand Sachem, 18, 123
Greeg, Thos., 91
Greenock, 20
Greenwich, x
Grenada, 29, 62, 69
Grenadine Keys, 62
Griffith, Edward, 87
Gross
  Mary, x
  Polly, xii
Guadaloupe, 29, 33
Guerriere, 6–7, 11
Halifax, 9, 15

Hamburg, James, 48
Hammond
 Mr., 99
 Thomas E., 50
Handee, Philip, 91
Hannah, 28, 33, 103, 123
Hardy, Beatriz B., v
Harmony, 105
Harriet Elizabeth, 104
Harris, William, 49
Haususon, John, 91
Havana, 15, 27, 70, 77–79, 81, 88, 97–100, 102, 118
Havanna, 74
Havre de Grace, France, 78
Havre de Grace, Maryland, 34
Hazard, 28, 123
Henry, 103
Henry of Hull, 10, 123
Henry, William, 50
Hester, x
Highflyer, 35, 42, 124
Hill, Jacob, 50
Hogan, John, 49
Hogues, William, 50
Holden, Peter, 11
Holkar, 124
Hollingsworth, Josse, 49
Holmes, Richard, 50
Holsom, Hamilton, 48
Holston, Hamilton, 100
Hooper, John, 11
Hopewell, 10–11, 103, 123
Hopkins, Fred W. Jr., x, 5, 25, 54, 57
Hoppings, Abraham, 51
Hornet, 9, 124
Horseshoe Bend, Alabama, Battle of, 26
Howe, John, 29
Hudson River, 26
Hull, 18
 Isaac, 7

Hurst, Adams, 51
Hutchinson, William, 36
Hyannis, Mass., 104
Impressment of American seamen, 1, 6
Industry, 11, 28–29, 33, 103, 123
Ingersoll, Jason, 32
Ironsides, Andrew, 91
Isaacs, 81
Itter, Capt., 68
Jackman, 28–29, 33, 103, 123
Jack's Favorite, 124
Jackson, Gen., 55
Jamaica, 70, 117
James, 21, 105, 118, 123
James, William, 35
Jane, 103
Java, 7, 13
Jefferson, John, 48
Joanna, 104
John, 12, 103
Jones, William, 50
Joseph & Mary, 124
Kay
 John, 91
 Mr., 90
Kelly, William, 91
Kelty, William, 48
Kemp
 James, 86
 Thomas, vii, ix, 5
Kerr, Charles, 87
Kilkadee, Scotland, 117
King, 73
Kingston, Jamaica, 72–73
La Plata, 118
Laguira, 31–32
Lake Champlain, 26
Lake Ontario, 13
Lamprey, 9, 123
Lankford, Ben, vii
Lanzarote, 117
Lark, 104

Lauter, Thos., 100
Lawrence, James, 14
Learlen, John, 91
Lennard, John, 48
Lewis, Charles, 49
Lexis, 123
Liauter, Thomas, 50
Liberty, 124
Linzee, 12
Lisbon, 9, 12, 18, 118
Liscure, Edward, 51
Little Belt, 6
Little Cayman Island, 73
Little Cherub, 28, 33, 103, 123
Liverpool, 18–19, 28, 118
London, 10–11, 37–38, 40, 69–70, 73, 117–118
London Convoy, 69–71
London Packet, 104
Long Island Sound, 14
Louis, 23, 123
Low, Philip, 51
Lucetta, 27, 123
Lutten, Lawrence, 49
Lye, C. J., 10–11
Mabo, Jos., 91
MacDonald, Janet, v
Macedonian, 7, 13
Maclay, Edgar Stanton, 38, 122
Madaira, 10, 123
Madeira Islands, 7
Madison, President James, x
Madrid, Spain, 7
Maffet, David, 37–38
Maffitt, David, 38–43
Majestic, 63
Malaga, 27
Many, 123
Marengo, 124
Marlborough, 27, 123
Marquis of Cornwallis, 105, 117
Mars, 32, 123
Martha, 104

Martin, 72, 105
Martinique, 29, 62, 67
Martys, Chas., 96
Mary, 29, 33, 62, 104–105
Mary & Susan, 105
Mary and Susanna, 73
Maryland Historical Society, v
Mason, Pierre A., 49
Matanzas, 88
Matanzes, 77–78
Mather, Mr., 90
McAdam, John, 55
McCombs, Solomon, 12
McConkey, John, 51, 58
McCulloch, Jas. U., 86
M'Connel, Samuel, 100
Mediterranean Sea, 15
Melponeene, 104
Messenger, 28, 33, 104, 123
Micus, 118
Middle Cape, 75–76
Miles, Jan, v
Miller, John, 50
Miranda, 104
Mississippi River, 14
Mohawk, 36
Mona, 71
Mona Passage, 33
Monk, Capt., 39
Montevideo, 15
Moore, George, 50
Moran
  Daniel, 48
  John, 50
  Mr., 99
Morant Point, 73
Morey, George, 36
Moroogon, William, 49
Morris, Richard, 6–7, 14
Moscow, Russia, 7
Nancy & Kate, 12, 123
Napoleon, 5, 7, 14, 26, 55
Narragansett, 34

National Road, 6
Naval History Center, v
Navy, U.S., 24–25
   advantages, 1–2
   number of ships in Atlantic theater, 1
   types of ships, 1
Nelson, Ed, v
Nemesis, 35, 42
Neversink, 57
New Bern, N.C., 26, 33, 36, 43, 104
New England, not blockaded, 34
New London, Conn., 7, 14
New Madrid Earthquake, 6
New Orleans, 32–33, 79, 98
   Battle of, 55, 61
New Orleans, steamboat, 6
New York, 14, 28, 32–33, 36, 39, 42, 45, 57, 85, 102, 105, 118
Newfoundland, 117–118
Newport, Rhode Island, 11, 104
Newton, 22–23, 123
Nicholas, John, 49
Nonesuch, 124
Norfolk, 15
Norfolk, Virginia, 34
North Point, 34
North River, 56
Nova Scotia, 7, 11
Nuestra Seno de Cormon, 27, 123
O'Hara, Robert, v
Okracoke, 36
Okracoke Harbor, 35
Okracoke Inlet, 42
   North Carolina, xi
Old Ironsides (Constitution), 8, 13
Old Point Comfort, 85
Oliver, 12
Oporto, 15, 20
Orders of Council, 124
Paris, 26
Patapsco, 25

Patriot, 124
Patterson, Nathaniel, 50
Patuxent River, 34
Paul Jones, 124
Pearson, John, 91
Pedro, Francisco, 49
Pelham, Henry, 48
Pelican, 24
Perkins, Jacob, 50
Pernambuco, 15, 17–18, 21, 121
philadelphia, 9
Philadelphia, 12, 18, 36, 39, 79, 98
Phoebe, 24
Phoenix, steamboat, 14
Pique, 32
Pircy, John, 51
Planter, 37–38, 40–41
Point Lookout, 85
Pomone, 63
Poole, 117
Port Royal, 14, 62
Port Saline, 64
Porter, David, 42
Porto Rico, 31–32, 72
Portsmouth, N.C., 36, 43
Portsmouth, N.H., 10
Powers, John, 69
Preciosa, 27, 123
President, 6, 9, 63
Pride of Baltimore, v, ix, 102, 120
Pride of Baltimore II, ix
Prince George's County, Maryland, Historical Society, v
Privateering, ix, x
Proffin, Elisabeth, v
Providence, x
Prudence, 105
Public Record Office, London, England, v
Puerto Rico, 71
Puffing Billy, 26
pursuit, 37
Pursuit, 38, 40–41

Raas, Thomas, 91
Rapp, Mr., 80
Ratliff, Henry, 49
Rattiff, John, 48
Rattray, James, 36
Recruit, 28, 123
Rees, Thomas, 94
Reindeer, 105, 117
Reiter, Michael, 50
Resolution, 12, 123
Retaliation, 124
Revenge, 25, 27, 123–124
Rhoads, Isaac, 50
Rice, Joseph, 49
Richardson, Joseph, 48
Richmond, 84
Right of Search, 124
Rio de Janiero, 17, 20
Roberts, George, 49
Rogers, John, 6
Rolla, ix, xii, 124
Rollinson, Thomas, 50
Romulus, 35, 42
Rosamond, 124
Rossie, ix, xii, 124
Rotterdam, 68
Rover, 124
royal george, 13
Royal Marine, 35
Royal Navy, 24, 34
   deficiencies, 2
   number of ships in Atlantic theater, 1
   types of ships in American waters, 1
Rush, Benjamin, 8
Saba, 27, 32
Sail Rock Passage, 27
Salamanca, Spain, 7
Salem, Mass., ix, xii
Sally, xii
Salvador, 19
Sandy Hook, 6, 56

Saphy, Thomas, 49
Sarah Ann, 124
Sarah Maria, 68
Saratoga, 124
Savannah, 14, 105
Scepter, 35
Scepter, 42
Scorpion, 36
Segourtney, Lt., 37
Selma, Thomas, 31
Seltzer, Don, v
Seth Long, 10
Severn, 102
Shaler, Nathaniel, 38, 42–43
Shannon, 14, 25
Shaw, James, 55
Sheads, Scott, v
Sheppard, Yankee, 51, 79, 100
Showmette, Donald, v
Siming, Henry, 49
Slaves, encouraged to defect, 35
Smith
   Capt., 18
   Thomas, 50
   William, 49
Sombrera, 27
Sombrero Passage, 23
Sommerset, William, 49
Southcomb, Kemp, 49
Spain, 34, 39
Spanish Town, Virgin Gorda, 31
Sparrow, 124
Speculator, 105
Spitfire, 6, 124
St. Anns, Jamaica, 73
St. Bartholomews, 21
St. Bartholomews (St Barthelemy), 22
St. Barts, 15, 27–29, 62, 68
St. Crois, 33
St. Croix, 10, 23–24, 31–32
St. David's Head, 24
St. Domingo, 71–72

St. Franciscus, 9, 123
St. Franciscus, 18
St. Helena, 55
St. Iago de Cuba, 75
St. John, 31
St. John, 33, 104
St. Johns, 20–21, 28, 32
St. Kitts, 23, 29, 33
St. Lawrence, xi, 43, 79, 81–82, 85, 87–97, 99–102, 105, 120–121
St. Lawrence, 36
St. Lucia, 29, 62, 64
St. Mary's County, Maryland, Historical Society, v
St. Michaels, xi, 15
St. Petersburg, 81
St. Pierre, 63
St. Thomas, 20–21, 27, 31–33, 74
St. Ubes, 11
St. Vincents, 28, 62, 64, 68
Stansbury, 20–21, 24
   Hamilton, 48
   James B., 5, 9
   N., 99
   Robert D., 50
Star Spangled Banner, 34
Staten Island, 56
Stephenson
   George, 55
   George P., 97
Stevens, John, 14
Stevenson, G.P., 99
Strategy, British and American, 1
Sullivan, Samuel H., 50
Surinam, 10–11, 28, 33, 38, 40
Surprise, 21, 123
Sutton, John, 48
Suvs, William, 49
Svennsson, Sam, 56
Swaggerer, 20–21, 123
Swanson, Richd, 91
Swordfish, 11, 123
Taber, Daniel, 49

Talbot County, Maryland, ix, xi
Tartar, 124
Teazer, 124
Tecumseh, 7, 14
Tenedos, 63
Tenefirre, 27
Thames, Ontario, Battle of, 14
Tharp
   J., 91
   James, 92
   Mr., 90, 93
Theodore, 105, 118
Theresa, x
Thompson, Theodore, 50
Tom, 124
Tonnant, 96
Tortola, 21, 27, 31
Tozer, Caleb Evans, 36
Traveller, x
Trinidad, 68
Tulip, 39
Turk's Island, 73
Tyler, Thomas, 51
Union, 124
United States, 7, 9, 13
United We Stand, 124
Valparaiso, Chile, 24
Venus, 27, 31–33, 104, 123
Vigilant, x, 29, 33, 104, 123
Vinard, E., 48
Vincent, Alfred, 100
Virginia, 7
Virginia Built Boat, viii
Virginia Capes, 25
Wake, Thomas N., 50
Walker, George, 48
Walter
   G., 91
   John, 93
   Mr., 94
Wanser, Henry, 49
War of 1812, 7
   reasons, 1

Ward, John, 63
Warren
  Sir John, 35
  Sir John Borlaise, 119
Wasa, 15, 123
Washington (City), 26, 63
  burned in 1814, 34
Wasp, 7, 25, 32, 62, 123–124
Waterloo, Battle of, 55
Weaver, Aquilla, 79, 100
Webb, Isaac, 48
Weeks
  Roberts, 50
  Thomas, 49
Wellington, 7, 55
West Indies, 56, 97, 102, 117, 120
West, Job, 27
Westhal, Lt., 35
Westphal, Lt., 42
Wheeler, John, 48
White
  Alexander P., 48, 100
  John, 49
  Samuel, 49
  William C., 49
Whitney, John, 50
Wild, Mr., 21
Wilder, Joseph, 50
William, 104
Williams, London, 48
Wilmington, 104
Wilmington, N.C., 26, 103–105
Wilson, Capt., 18
Wiltberger, Joseph S., 50
Wolf Trap, 85
Yankee, 21, 123
Yellow fever, 29
Yeocomico River, 36
York (Toronto), 14
Yorktown, 124
Young, Samuel, 49

www.ingramcontent.com/pod-product-compliance
Lightning Source LLC
Chambersburg PA
CBHW071503180426
43194CB00051B/1735